Twayne's English Authors Series

EDITOR OF THIS VOLUME

Bertram H. Davis

Florida State University

Susanna Centlivre

TEAS 254

Susanna Centlivre

SUSANNA CENTLIVRE

By F. P. LOCK
University of Queensland

TWAYNE PUBLISHERS
A DIVISION OF G. K. HALL & CO., BOSTON

Published in 1979 by Twayne Publishers,
A Division of G. K. Hall & Co.
All Rights Reserved

Printed on permanent/durable acid-free paper and bound
in the United States of America

First Printing

Library of Congress Cataloging in Publication Data

Lock, F. P.
Susanna Centlivre.

(Twayne's English authors series)
Bibliography: p. 146-52
Includes index.
1. Centlivre, Susanna, 1667?-1723—Criticism and
interpretation.
PR3339.C6L6   1979   822'.5   78-24405
ISBN 0-8057-6744-4

Contents

About the Author

F. P. Lock was born in England in 1948 and received his B.A. from the University of Cambridge in 1971. From 1971 to 1974 he was a Dalley Fellow at McMaster University, Canada, where he received his M.A. in 1972 and his Ph.D. in 1975. Since 1974 he has taught in the Department of English at the University of Queensland, Australia. In 1978 he was an Andrew W. Mellon Fellow at the Clark Library, University of California at Los Angeles. He has edited James Bramston's *The Man of Taste* (1733) for the Augustan Reprint Society (Los Angeles, 1975). His essay on Centlivre's precursors, "Astraea's 'Vacant Throne': The Successors of Aphra Behn" appeared in *Woman in the Eighteenth Century and Other Essays*, ed. Paul Fritz and Richard Morton (Toronto, 1976). He was also co-author (with Alan Lawson) of *Australian Literature: A Reference Guide* (Melbourne, 1977). He has also contributed articles and notes on Chaucer, eighteenth-century drama, and Jane Austen to the *Book Collector*, *Eighteenth Century Studies*, *English Language Notes*, *Notes and Queries*, the *Transactions of the Cambridge Bibliographical Society*, and the *Yearbook of English Studies*. His major current interests are in restoration and eighteenth-century drama and in the relations of literature, politics, and ideas in the early eighteenth century.

Preface

Susanna Centlivre was one of the leading comic dramatists of the early eighteenth century. Most histories and studies of the drama and theater of the period give some space to her and her plays. But there has never been a full critical study of her work. Only one previous book has been written about her: John Wilson Bowyer's *The Celebrated Mrs. Centlivre* (1952), based on his Harvard dissertation (1928). Bowyer's valuable work remains the essential starting point for the study of Centlivre. He assembled almost all the relevant sources and allusions, providing a very thorough survey of Centlivre's life and writings. Not much new evidence has come to light since Bowyer wrote, and I have drawn most of my facts, especially about Centlivre's life, from his book. But Bowyer is weak on critical judgments: his book is a literary biography rather than a critical study.

The emphasis of this book is literary rather than biographical, and critical rather than historical. It is primarily an analytical study of Centlivre's plays, although it also takes into account the historical context in which they were written. The English dramatists of the early eighteenth century naturally had much in common. They lived in the same great city and wrote largely for the same audiences. They responded to the same political events and social pressures and changes. On the other hand, they were also individuals. Centlivre was sometimes an opportunist, but at her best she maintained an individual and authentic voice. I have tried to bring out her distinctive qualities in this study.

Biographical details and problems, Centlivre's friends, and her political and critical ideas are the subject of Chapter 1. A detailed critical study of Centlivre's plays extends over the next six chapters. No uniformity of scale or treatment has been imposed: the method is varied to suit each play. This extensive treatment of the plays is complemented by a much briefer survey, in Chapter 8, of Centlivre's letters and verse. Finally, there is an assessment of Centlivre's achievement and her place in the English dramatic tradition. Much more could have been said about the staging and stage histories of the

plays: but that would have made a different book, primarily of interest
to theater historians. More could also have been written about the
sources of Centlivre's plays: but except where they illustrate a critical
point, I have not discussed them in detail. The various scholars who
first pointed out Centlivre's borrowings will be found in Bowyer.

There is no modern edition of Centlivre's plays nor have her
nondramatic writings ever been collected. Thalia Stathas has edited
A Bold Stroke for a Wife for the Regents Restoration Drama Series
(1968). I have used this edition, but for all Centlivre's other works I
have relied on the first editions. Notes have been kept to a minimum
by identifying quotations from, and references to, Centlivre's works
by inserting page numbers in the text. These refer either to the first
edition, or to Stathas in the case of *A Bold Stroke for a Wife*. There are
some irregularities in the pagination of some of the first editions:
details are recorded in the Selected Bibliography. No references are
given for dedications, prefaces, prologues, or epilogues. These
usually appear on unnumbered pages, and they are easy enough to
locate. Quotations retain the spelling and punctuation of the original,
with the following exceptions: obvious misprints are corrected, the
long s is eliminated, and the use of italics is brought into conformity
with modern usage. In quoting dialogue, I have expanded and
regularized speech prefixes. I have also, in the text, modernized the
titles of Centlivre's plays. There seemed no reason to prefer *The
Perjur'd Husband* to *The Perjured Husband*. The original forms will
be found in the Selected Bibliography.

My most important scholarly debts are to Bowyer's *The Celebrated
Mrs. Centlivre*; to Avery's *The London Stage, Part 2*; and to Norton's
bibliography of Centlivre in the *Book Collector*. Bowyer I have cited
throughout simply by name. All information about the contemporary
performances of Centlivre's plays is taken from Avery; the date serves
as a reference. Dates of publication are taken from Norton. I have
used many other sources, of course; details are recorded in the Notes
and References and in the Selected Bibliography.

F. P. LOCK

University of Queensland

Chronology

1669 November 20: Susanna, daughter of William Freeman, baptized in the parish church of Whaplode, Lincolnshire.

1674 June 23: Edward Freeman of Holbeach, Lincolnshire, left twenty shillings to his daughter Susanna.

1681 (?) Orphaned by the death of her mother.

1684 (?) Married a nephew of Sir Stephen Fox.

1685 (?) After the death (?) of her first husband, married an army officer named Carroll.

1687 (?) Widowed a second time.

1700 By March of this year, had settled in London and made the acquaintance of some writers. She first appeared in print in a collection of *Familiar and Courtly Letters*, published May 11. Her first play, *The Perjured Husband*, was produced at Drury Lane in the fall and published October 22.

1701 Further correspondence appeared in *Familiar and Courtly Letters*, Vol. II (May), and in *Letters of Wit, Politics, and Morality* (July).

1702 May: England declared war on France and Spain. Enthusiasm for the war reflected in *The Beau's Duel*, produced at Lincoln's Inn Fields about June (published July 8). *The Stolen Heiress* produced at the same theater December 31 (published anonymously, January 19, 1703).

1703 *Love's Contrivance* produced at Drury Lane June 4 (published June 14, with a Dedication signed "R. M.").

1705 First popular success, *The Gamester*, produced at Lincoln's Inn Fields in January (published anonymously, February 22). *The Basset Table* produced at Drury Lane November 20 (published November 21, as "by the Author of *The Gamester*").

1706 *Love at a Venture* produced at Bath by a traveling company, the Duke of Grafton's Men. The troupe also acted before the court at Windsor, where Susanna met Joseph Centlivre, one of the royal cooks. *Love at a Venture* published in London as "by the Author of *The Gamester*." *The Platonic Lady* produced at the Queen's Theater November 25 and published December 9.

1707 April 23: Married Joseph Centlivre.

1709 *The Busy Body* produced at Drury Lane May 12 and published May 31, under Centlivre's own name—as were all her subsequent plays. *The Man's Bewitched* produced at the Queen's Theater December 12 (published December 31).

1710 *A Bickerstaff's Burying* produced at Drury Lane March 27 (published December 26). *Marplot,* a sequel to *The Busy Body,* produced at Drury Lane December 30 (published January 10, 1711).

1712 *The Perplexed Lovers* Produced at Drury Lane January 19.

1713 March: The Peace of Utrecht ended the War of the Spanish Succession. The Centlivres moved to Buckingham Court, near Charing Cross, their home for the rest of Susanna's life. Her poem *The Masquerade* published September 3.

1714 April: The "Cambridge writ" affair. *The Wonder* produced at Drury Lane April 27; published in May. August 1: Death of Queen Anne; George I proclaimed king. Centlivre celebrated the new dynasty in two poems: *A Poem Humbly Presented to His Most Sacred Majesty* (published November 7) and *An Epistle to Mrs. Wallup* (published November 14).

1715 June: Two farces—*The Gotham Election* and *A Wife Well Managed*—published after the Lord Chamberlain refused to license them for the stage.

1716 Centlivre included by Pope in his attacks on Edmund Curll and his authors. *The Cruel Gift* produced at Drury Lane December 17 (published January 3, 1717).

1717 *Three Hours after Marriage,* a farce by Gay, Pope, and Arbuthnot, produced at Drury Lane in January: Centlivre satirized through the character of Phoebe Clinket. Centlivre's *Epistle to the King of Sweden* published March 12.

1718 *A Bold Stroke for a Wife* produced at Lincoln's Inn Fields February 3 (published February 28).

1719 Centlivre seriously ill.

1720 *A Woman's Case* published about July. A series of political abstracts contributed to the *Weekly Journal* from September to December. An engraved portrait of Centlivre published in London October 29.

1722 *The Artifice* produced at Drury Lane October 2 (published October 27).

1723　December 1: died; buried in St. Paul's, Covent Garden.

1724　A *Wife Well Managed* produced at the Haymarket May 2. Joseph Centlivre died (his will proved January 21, 1725).

1732　A four volume edition of Centlivre's *Dramatical Works*, with "some Account of her Life and Writings. By her self" advertised, but apparently not published.

1760　Centlivre's plays finally collected in a three volume edition of *Works* (dated 1760–1761).

CHAPTER 1

Introduction

S USANNA Centlivre was a minor celebrity in the literary world of
her day, when a woman writer was still conspicuous by the very
fact of her sex. She wrote nineteen plays, numerous poems, and some
witty love letters. After an unsettled youth—the details of which are
lost in obscurity—she enjoyed a respectable middle age as the wife of
one of the royal cooks. In politics she was a zealous Whig, and after
1712 a vocal one. Her friends included such like-minded writers as
Richard Steele, Nicholas Rowe, and Ambrose Philips. Pope, however, regarded her as a scribbler and gave her a posthumous niche in
The Dunciad. She died in 1723, aged about fifty-four. Although her
plays never commanded much critical respect, three of them—*The
Busy Body, The Wonder,* and *A Bold Stroke for a Wife*—enjoyed a
long life in the repertory of the popular theater.

I *Biographical Problems*

We can trace Centlivre's literary career in detail. But her early
years, before her arrival in London in 1700, are obscure, and personal
details about even her later life are scanty. The early biographies are
incomplete, inaccurate, and inconsistent with each other. The most
reliable accounts are those that are based, wholly or in part, on
firsthand knowledge or recollection. There are four of these: by Giles
Jacob (1719), Abel Boyer (1723), John Mottley (1747), and William
Rufus Chetwood (1750).[1]

The earliest, the most authoritative, and the only source that
appeared in Centlivre's lifetime is the article on her in Giles Jacob's
literary reference work, *The Poetical Register* (1719). In the Preface,
Jacob claims that most of the biographical material about living
authors "came from their own Hands." Omitting his list of Centlivre's
plays, Jacob's sketch of her life is as follows:

This Gentlewoman, now living, is Daughter of one Mr. Freeman, late of Holbeach, in Lincolnshire, who married a Daughter of Mr. Marham, a Gentleman of a good Estate at Lynn Regis, in the County of Norfolk. There was formerly an Estate in the Family of her Father; but he being a Dissenter, and a zealous Parliamentarian, was so very much persecuted at the Restoration, that he was necessitated to fly into Ireland, and his Estate was confiscated: Nor was the Family of her Mother free from the Severities of those Times, they being likewise Parliamentarians. Her Education was in the Country; and her Father dying when she was but three Years of Age; and her Mother not living till she was twelve, what Improvements she has made, have been meerly by her own Industry and Application. She was married before the Age of Fifteen, to a Nephew of Sir Stephen Fox. This Gentleman living with her but a Year, she afterwards married Mr. Carrol, an Officer in the Army: And survived him likewise, in the space of a Year and a half. She is since married to Mr. Joseph Cent Livre, Yeoman of the Mouth to his present Majesty. She was inclin'd to Poetry when very Young, having compos'd a Song before she was Seven Years old. She has wrote Fifteen Plays; her Talent is Comedy, particularly in the Contrivance of the Plots and Incidents; the Conduct and Beauty of which, are sufficiently recommended by Sir Richard Steele, in one of the *Spectator's*.[2]

Several considerations make it appear plausible that Jacob received his information from Centlivre herself. There is the mention of the precocious song; and there is the conspicuous lack of any reference to the "gay Adventures" of her youth that we find in all the other sources. At several points, the clever phrasing seems designed to mislead without actually telling a direct untruth. It is not clear why the estate is vaguely described as being "in the family" of her father; why we are left ignorant of her first husband's name, but told who his uncle was; whether this nephew actually died after "living with her but a Year"; and if he did not, in what sense Susanna survived Carroll "likewise." The sketch raises as many questions as it answers. If it is all true, it does not sound like the whole truth.

When Centlivre died in 1723, several obituaries appeared in the newspapers. A more substantial one was written by Abel Boyer, the Whig historian and journalist, for his monthly review, *The Political State of Great Britain*. Boyer had been friendly with Centlivre in 1701, when she contributed to a collection of letters that he edited. They were both Whigs, but we do not know how closely they kept in touch with each other between 1701 and 1723. The biographical part of Boyer's obituary is as follows:

The same Day [December 1, 1723], died also Mrs. Susannah Centlivre, Wife to Joseph Centlivre, one of the Yeomen of the Kitchen to his Majesty. Her Father's Name, if I mistake not, was Rawkins, her first Husband's, Carol. From a mean Parentage, and Education, after several gay Adventures (over which we shall draw a Veil) she had, at last, so well improved her natural Genius, by Reading and good Conversation, as to attempt to write for the stage; in which she had as good Success, as any of her Sex before her.[3]

Boyer's confusion about names is understandable at the distance of so many years. "Rawkins" is certainly not a figment of his imagination. The dramatist is described as "Susannah Caroll als Rawkins" in the license for her marriage to Joseph Centlivre.[4] Nor can Boyer's statement about her "mean Parentage" be lightly dismissed; he may have made a mistake, but it is hardly likely that he would tell a deliberate lie. It is more probable that Centlivre stretched the truth when she told Jacob that there had been an estate "in the Family" of her father.

Boyer's reticence about the "gay Adventures" was not imitated by John Mottley, who is generally credited—on internal evidence— with authorship of the *Complete List of All the English Dramatic Poets* appended to Thomas Whincop's *Scanderbeg* (1747). The article on Centlivre in this work is a curious amalgam of apparently authentic detail and improbable apocryphal anecdote. Mottley was living in London during the second half of Centlivre's career, and according to his own account, he assisted her with the writing of *A Bold Stroke for a Wife* (1718). Mottley includes details about presents given to Centlivre by her patrons that he can only have derived from the dramatist herself. He also gives a believable character sketch: "If she had not a great deal of Wit in her Conversation, she had much Vivacity and good Humour; she was remarkably good-natured and benevolent in her Temper, and ready to do any friendly Office as far as it was in her Power."[5] But Mottley's most striking, and least credible, contribution to the Centlivre story is an adventure that he relates between her leaving home and her first marriage. It is a good story, but Mottley himself hardly expects us to believe it. He introduces it with the saving clause, "if we may give Credit to some private Stories concerning her."[6] According to Mottley, Susanna left home to escape the cruelty of a stepmother. Weeping at the roadside, she was picked up by a Cambridge student (Anthony Hammond, future M.P., man of affairs, and minor poet), disguised as his "Cousin Jack," and installed in his college rooms. The imposture, and Susanna's university education, were prolonged for some months. At length, Hammond sent her away to seek her fame and fortune in London. Mottley places the incident before the first two "marriages," which he goes out of his way to discredit. He describes her as "married, or something like it" to the nephew of Sir Stephen Fox, whom Carroll merely "succeeded in her Affections."[7] The Hammond episode obviously cannot be accepted as it stands. It may be pure fiction, or it may be a much improved version of something that really happened. We would certainly be less willing to credit Mottley's doubts about the early "marriages" if it were not for the studied ambiguity of Jacob's account. Mottley seems reliable on Centlivre's later years, but talking about her early life he is "only too obviously anxious to tell a lively story."[8] This does not mean that everything he says must be discounted; but it is hard to separate fact from fiction.

A fourth source that may be based on firsthand knowledge is the brief account in William Rufus Chetwood's *The British Theatre* (1750). Chetwood was, toward the end of Centlivre's career, successively a bookseller with theatrical interests and (from 1722) prompter at Drury Lane. If he did not already know Centlivre, he would most likely have made her acquaintance when *The Artifice* was produced at Drury Lane in October 1722. Chetwood confirms that her father's name was Freeman and describes her family as "Reputable." But his main contribution is a more circumstantial account of her education and an alternative sequence of "gay Adventures." Her education he ascribes "intirely to her own Industry, and the Assistance of a Neighbouring French Gentleman, who so much admired her sprightly Wit and Manner, that he undertook to instruct her in the French Language."[9] As a result, she acquired an early taste for Molière. Chetwood agrees with Mottley that she left home to escape the ill usage of a stepmother: but he has her join a company of strolling players, a more probable if less romantic adventure than Mottley's roadside drama. Chetwood follows Boyer's reticence and decides to "drop her Marriages, and Amours."[10] Chetwood may have received some information from Centlivre herself, although that would be no guarantee of its veracity; in any case, we would have to allow for the tricks of memory natural after a lapse of thirty years.

It seems likely that there is some substance to the "gay Adventures" attested by Boyer, Mottley, and Chetwood. But there is too much improbability and inconsistency in their accounts for us to reconstruct them in detail. Centlivre herself was evidently anxious to prevent such stories from becoming public. Why the unscrupulous publisher Edmund Curll did not issue one of his notorious "lives" on Centlivre has always been a puzzle. If stories such as Boyer knew were current, Curll's restraint is the more remarkable.

Documentary evidence is not much help in settling these biographical problems. It chiefly concerns her birth, her marriage to Centlivre, and her death. The future dramatist was probably the Susanna, daughter of William and Anne Freeman, who was baptized in the parish church of Whaplode, Lincolnshire, on November 20, 1669.[11] Whaplode is close to Holbeach, where Jacob places her family. But another Susanna was left twenty shillings in the will of her father, Edward Freeman, of Holbeach itself, whose will was proved on June 23, 1674.[12] This would be about the time that Susanna's father would have died if Jacob's account is correct. But since the will directs that payments are to be made within a year, this Susanna was probably not a child at the time.[13] This consideration inclines the balance in favor of the Whaplode Freeman being the dramatist's father. No record has been traced of Centlivre's first two supposed marriages, to the nephew of Sir Stephen Fox and Mr. Carroll (whose name is variously spelled). Her third marriage, to Joseph Centlivre, took place on April 23, 1707.[14] Her death on December 1, 1723, and her burial in St. Paul's, Covent Garden, on December 4, are also documented.[15]

Perhaps the truth is somewhere between the undeserved hardships chronicled by Jacob and the "gay Adventures" alluded to by Boyer and Chetwood and elaborated by Mottley. It seems most likely that she was orphaned, since we hear nothing of her family or connections in her later life, although we know that she revisited Holbeach on more than one occasion.[16] These visits would be a natural result of what Dr. Johnson was to call everyone's "lurking wish to appear considerable in his native place."[17] All the sources agree that Centlivre received little or no formal education and was accustomed to independence from an early age. Perhaps one of the most puzzling questions is why, if she was indeed born in 1669, she did not come to London before 1700. This would have been the obvious destination for an ambitious girl conscious of her abilities but without either friends or connections.

After 1700 we have a full record of Centlivre's literary career, although there is still little personal evidence. But we know who many of her friends and acquaintances were and therefore something of the social life she led. If her early life remains obscure, that obscurity is itself significant in an age when birth and fortune counted for more than ability in the business of getting on in life. All her early biographers agree that she owed her success and her reputation entirely to her own talents and efforts.

II   Earning a Living

Writing plays was not a very profitable occupation in Queen Anne's London. George Farquhar died in poverty in 1707, after writing two popular successes in less than two years. Jane Wiseman, whose tragedy *Antiochus the Great* was produced at Drury Lane in 1702, subsequently "married a young Vintner . . . and with the Profits arising from her Play, they set up a Tavern in Westminister".[18] It was evidently more prudent to trust Bacchus than Apollo. Before she married Joseph Centlivre in 1707, Susanna wrote for a living. In the six years that she had been in London, eight of her plays had been produced. But only one had been a real success, and in 1706 she was driven to the expedient of joining a company of traveling actors. She would only have done so from financial necessity.

As a dramatist, she had three possible sources of income: theatrical benefits, sale of copyright, and patronage. Unfortunately, no receipts are recorded for any contemporary performances of her plays, so it is not easy to estimate her income from them. On the third and sixth nights of a new play—supposing that it lasted so long—she would receive the night's receipts, less a deduction (about £40 at this time) for the theater's operating costs. She would also keep any money that she had collected from the sale of tickets to her friends and acquaintances. Of Centlivre's first eight plays, only *The Gamester* reached a sixth night. We have more precise information about the sale of her copyrights. Bernard Lintot paid £10 each for *Love's Contrivance* and *The Busy Body*. With the possible exception of *The Gamester*, it is not likely that she received more for any of her early plays. Later, Edmund Curll paid £21 each for *The Wonder, The Cruel Gift,* and *The Artifice.*[19] It is difficult to generalize about patronage. The patron to whom a play was dedicated might give a considerable present or nothing at all. According to Mottley, Eustace Budgell gave Centlivre "a Diamond Ring worth about twenty Guineas" when she dedicated *The Cruel Gift* to him.[20] Altogether, Centlivre might have grossed anything from £50 to £100 from those of her early plays that reached at least a third night and perhaps from £100 to £150 from her more successful later ones.[21] How well she could live on these receipts would depend entirely on how frugal or extravagant she chose to be.[22]

Her tour with the traveling actors in 1706 had a decisive effect on Centlivre's career. According to Mottley, it was while acting before the court at Windsor that Susanna met Joseph Centlivre.[23] After their marriage in 1707, she naturally enjoyed much greater social and financial security. This had its effect on her plays, which after 1707 were more original. Joseph Centlivre's place as Yeoman of the Mouth—a middle-ranking position in the hierarchy of the royal kitchen—paid £60 per year, with the perquisite of £1 6s from every new knight.[24] If Susanna had kept up her earlier output, their combined income might have reached £200. After her marriage, however, Centlivre was less prolific. This suggests that financial pressures were partly responsible for some of her early plays, especially such hasty compilations as *The Stolen Heiress* and *Love's Contrivance*.

But if after 1707 Centlivre wrote with more freedom and wrote more slowly, she was not for that reason less interested in popular success. Throughout her career, she continued to write to please her audience. The slowing down indicates that she could now afford to take more time to write a better play: her three best plays were all written after her marriage to Centlivre. That she wrote for a living does not imply that she had no artistic conscience: but certainly after 1707 she was less constrained in the exercise of it.

III *Friends*

Through her husband's position, Centlivre would have come into contact with the belowstairs life of the court. She herself belonged to the belowstairs life of the literary world.[25] Her friends were not the great writers of the day, but were drawn instead from the middling ranks of authors and even from the confines of Grub Street. In her first years in London, she knew William Ayloffe, Abel Boyer, Tom Brown, George Farquhar, Jane Wiseman, and no doubt others. The writers named are her correspondents in the collections of letters to which she contributed in 1700 and 1701. The most considerable of the group is certainly Farquhar. *The Constant Couple* (1699) had already made him a popular dramatist. If the letters are not entirely fictional, Farquhar was intent on an affair with Susanna. Apparently she preferred their friendship to remain an intellectual one.[26] Abel Boyer and Jane Wiseman have already been mentioned. In 1701 Boyer, a

Huguenot refugee, was chiefly known as the author of a French-English dictionary. Ayloffe and Brown were men about town and miscellaneous writers. By 1705 Susanna was also on friendly terms with two other women writers: Mary Pix, the dramatist; and Sarah Fyge Egerton, the poet. By the same year she also knew Nicholas Rowe and Charles Johnson. Rowe was already a successful tragic dramatist, although not yet poet laureate; Johnson was another dramatist of Whig sympathies. Rowe wrote the Prologue, and Johnson the Epilogue, for *The Gamester.*

Several other writers contributed prologues and epilogues for Centlivre's later plays. Some, published as "By a Gentleman," are still unidentified. Allardyce Nicoll has suggested that the "Mr. B—" who wrote the Epilogue for *The Perjured Husband* was William Burnaby, the dramatist.[27] Farquhar wrote the Prologue for *The Platonic Lady;* another dramatist, Thomas Baker, wrote an Epilogue that "came too late" to be used. Promises of such favors could not be relied upon: Baker's Prologue for *The Busy Body* arrived on time, but the Epilogue promised by Richard Steele never arrived at all—despite her reminder in the form of a verse epistle. Steele made some amends by praising *The Busy Body* in the *Tatler.* Centlivre and he remained on friendly terms: in 1714 he praised *The Wonder* in his current periodical the *Lover,* and Centlivre asked his advice—although she did not take it—on the question of dedicating the play. Colley Cibber was certainly not one of Centlivre's friends, but he wrote the Epilogue for *The Man's Bewitched.* Possibly he was making amends for his previous ill-treatment of Centlivre: in 1706 he had rejected *Love at a Venture* when it was offered to Drury Lane, yet the next year he stole part of the play for his own *Double Gallant.*

Ambrose Philips, pastoral poet, dramatist, and Whig, wrote the Epilogue for *The Wonder.* Another Whig wit, Thomas Burnet, son of the bishop of Salisbury, supplied the Prologue. Nicholas Rowe contributed an Epilogue for *The Cruel Gift,* and according to Mottley, he also "gave some slight Touches to the Play."[28] George Sewell, the "controversialist and hack-writer" as the *Dictionary of National Biography* succinctly styles him, wrote the Epilogues for *A Bold Stroke for a Wife* and for *The Artifice.* William Bond, a minor poet, wrote the Prologue for *The Artifice.* John Mottley, by his own account, assisted Centlivre with *A Bold Stroke for a Wife,* writing "one or two entire Scenes of it."[29] When Centlivre dedicated *The Cruel Gift* to Eustace Budgell, she claimed him as a friend. Budgell is best known as Addison's cousin and as a contributor to the *Spectator.*

None of Centlivre's other dedications imply personal friendship. Two other minor poets, Anthony Hammond and Nicholas Amhurst, addressed poems to Centlivre in the *New Miscellany of Original Poems* (1720)—a volume which Hammond edited and to which Centlivre contributed. Hammond will be remembered as the hero of Mottley's roadside romance.

Most of the writers mentioned were well-known for their Whig sympathies. Steele is the most prominent, in politics as in literature, but Burnet, Johnson, and Philips all belonged to the circle that gathered around Addison at Button's Coffeehouse. Boyer was a Whig apologist. Amhurst was later editor of the Tory *Craftsman*, but when Centlivre knew him he was a Whig. Conversely, George Sewell had been a Tory, but in 1718 he attached himself to Walpole and the Whigs. Rowe's tragedy *Tamerlane* (1701) was regarded as the classic dramatic exposition of the Whig theory of constitutional monarchy.[30] Less flatteringly, many of these writers found themselves—along with Centlivre herself—on the wrong side of Pope's satire. The following can be found in *The Dunciad*: Bond, Boyer, Budgell, Burnet, Cibber, Johnson, Philips, and—in an early draft—Pix. Some owed their inclusion to their politics, some to their bad writing: some, like Centlivre herself, to both. But to take such writers at Pope's valuation of them is to distort literary history. In 1714 it was no disgrace to number among one's friends Budgell, Johnson, Philips, Rowe, and Steele. If Centlivre did not move in the most aristocratic literary circles, she had a group of friends who would take her seriously as a writer and whose society would be a valued source of criticism, encouragement, and example.

IV *Politics*

The early eighteenth century was an age of political deviousness and double dealing, but there is nothing doubtful or obscure about Centlivre's political convictions. Throughout her life and in her writings, she was a firm and ardent supporter of the Whigs. She may have inherited these principles from her father. Jacob describes him as a "Dissenter, and a zealous Parliamentarian" who was "very much persecuted at the Restoration".[31] Centlivre's political views rarely found direct expression in her plays, except through incidental remarks that are usually patriotic rather than party-political. Her only play that is actually about politics is *The Gotham Election* and this was refused a license by the Lord Chamberlain. The theaters were by no means unregulated before the famous Licensing Act of 1737. There is, however, plenty of evidence in Centlivre's poems, and in her dedications, prologues, and epilogues, for us to document her views on the major political questions that divided the nation: the war and the succession.

The War of the Spanish Succession lasted from 1702 to 1713. Initially it was supported by both Whigs and Tories. Centlivre expressed her enthusiasm for it in *The Beau's Duel*, which was produced in June 1702, a month after the outbreak of the war. She made the two heroes of the play soldiers and introduced a recruiting scene in which a coward, Ogle, is frightened out of his rash military ambitions. But after about 1708 the war became less popular, and Centlivre's continued support for it assumed less a patriotic and more a party complexion. The Whigs continued to support the war; the Tories clamored for a peace. Early in 1709, peace negotiations were begun at The Hague. Thomas Baker, a dramatist without strong political loyalties to either party, represented the popular mood in the Prologue that he wrote for Centlivre's new play, *The Busy Body*, which was produced on May 12, 1709:

> Undaunted Collonels will to Camps repair,
> Assur'd, there'll be no Skirmishes this Year;
> On our own Terms will flow the wish'd-for Peace,
> All Wars, except 'twixt Man and Wife, will cease.

The Epilogue, written by Centlivre herself, is notably less enthusiastic about the prospective peace:

> Some snivling Cits, wou'd have a Peace for spight,
> To starve those Warriours who so bravely fight.
> Still of a Foe upon his Knees affraid;
> Whose well-bang'd Troops want Money, Heart, and Bread.

In the event, the peace terms were rejected by the French king, and there was a campaign. Marlborough won another victory at Malplaquet, but the war became increasingly unpopular in England.

During 1710 most of the Whigs were removed from office, and the general election in October returned a large Tory majority in support of a government now pledged to end the war. In January 1712, Prince Eugene of Savoy arrived in England on a diplomatic mission on behalf of the allies. Eugene found himself welcomed, for different reasons, by both parties: "The Whigs praised him as the friend and partner in war of their injured hero [Marlborough], come over to help him avert a disgraceful peace. The Tories hailed him no less loudly, as a greater general and a nobler man than Marlborough."[32]

Centlivre's new comedy, *The Perplexed Lovers,* was produced at Drury Lane on January 19. The comedy itself was unexceptionable, but a political allusion in the Epilogue ran into trouble. The part of the Epilogue that gave offense was a reference to Marlborough, praising him—he is the *"ONE"* in the lines quoted—equally with Prince Eugene:

> Such as that Stranger who has grac'd our Land,
> Of equal Fame for Council, and Command.
> A Prince, whose Wisdom, Valour, and Success,
> The gazing World with Acclamations bless;
> By no great Captain in past Times outdone,
> And in the present equal'd but by *ONE.*

Marlborough was out of favor with the Tory government; he had recently been dismissed from all his official positions. Centlivre could not get the Epilogue licensed in time for the opening night of the play, and the managers of the theater thought it imprudent to have it spoken without a license. The Epilogue was licensed the next day, but by this time—as Centlivre tells us in her Preface—a rumor had spread that it was a "notorious whiggish" one. Mrs. Oldfield, who was to have spoken the Epilogue, was advised that a claque was being formed against it. A substitute Epilogue was spoken instead. The offending Epilogue was published with the play on February 22. Centlivre also printed with the play a poem dedicated to Prince Eugene and a Preface in which she indignantly described the undeserved misfortunes of the original Epilogue. She professed not to be able to understand how the Epilogue could be construed as Whiggish: "I know not what they call Whigs, or how they distinguish between them and Tories: But if the Desire to see my Country secur'd from the Romish Yoke, and flourish by a Firm Lasting Honourable Peace, to the Glory of the best of Queens . . . be a Whig, then I am one, else not." This was Centlivre's first outspoken statement of her political credo. In the event, Eugene's mission achieved nothing. The Peace of Utrecht was concluded in 1713: but it was not what Centlivre and the Whigs regarded as a "Firm Lasting Honourable" one.

The next major issue was the succession to the throne. This

assumed a new urgency when Queen Anne fell dangerously ill in December 1713. The Tory government was officially committed to the Act of Settlement of 1701, which excluded Catholics from the throne and fixed the succession on the protestant House of Hanover. But many Tories were also Jacobites: that is, supporters of the Stuarts. They wished Anne to be succeeded by her half-brother, "James III." Some members of the government, especially Secretary Bolingbroke, were thought to favor—and even to be plotting—a Jacobite restoration on Anne's death. In April 1714, both Houses of Parliament voted (but only by narrow margins), the protestant succession not in danger under the Tory government. The heir to the throne was the elderly Dowager Electress Sophia of Hanover. Her grandson, the future George II, had been given an English peerage with the title Duke of Cambridge. Throughout Anne's reign there had been proposals to invite a member of the electoral family to England; but Anne herself had always been strongly against the idea. On April 12, 1714, Schütz—the Hanoverian envoy in London— requested a writ to call the Duke of Cambridge to the House of Lords. The writ was issued after a stormy cabinet session, but it was made clear that the queen did not want the duke to come to England. Possibly the request for the writ was a tactical error; but support for the "Cambridge writ" soon became a touchstone for commitment to the protestant succession.

On April 27, Centlivre's new comedy, *The Wonder,* was produced at Drury Lane. Obviously it had been written long before the writ became a political issue, and the play itself is not concerned with politics. But Centlivre made the play political by dedicating it to the Duke of Cambridge when it was published in May. In the Dedication, Centlivre wrote of the impatience with which she and other loyal Britons were awaiting the duke's arrival and anticipated English liberties being secured under a protestant and Hanoverian succession. The Dedication was a bold move politically: Steele apparently advised against it. In the event, the gamble paid off handsomely: Jacobite hopes evaporated when Queen Anne died on August 1 and—Sophia having died shortly before Anne—George I was proclaimed without opposition. Centlivre's loyalty was not forgotten. When the Duke of Cambridge—now Prince of Wales—arrived in England, he commanded a performance of *The Wonder* (December 16, 1714), and according to Mottley he "made the Author an handsome Present".[33] This was not the end of royal patronage of Centlivre's plays. In 1717, the prince commanded performances of

The Cruel Gift (May 3) and of *The Busy Body* (October 23). On March 17, 1720, the king himself commanded a performance of *The Busy Body* for the author's benefit.

As we would expect, Centlivre celebrated the Hanoverian succession in several poems. Nor did her expressions of loyalty end with the dynasty's establishment. There is no need to review them here; they are all listed in the bibliography, and the more important ones discussed in Chapter 8.

V *Critical Ideas*

Centlivre's critical ideas were expressed with less force and consistency than her political convictions. Obviously she was more dependent on the vagaries of public taste in what she wrote, while she could please herself in what she thought. For the greater part of her career, in dedications, prefaces, prologues, and epilogues, she reiterated her belief that the business of comedy was to entertain. Because she had an important financial interest in the success of her plays, this aim to please took priority over instructing the audience and following the rules. In the Preface to *Love's Contrivance* (1703), indeed, she pays lip service to the three unities as "the greatest Beauties of a Dramatick Poem." But because the audience "relishes nothing so well as Humour lightly tost up with Wit, and drest with Modesty and Air," even here she rejects the unities in favor of the "other way of writing" which "pleases full as well, and gives the Poet a larger Scope of Fancy, and with less Trouble, Care, and Pains, serves his and the Players End." This disregard for the rules in the interest of pleasing is reminiscent of Farquhar's "Discourse upon Comedy" (1702). But Centlivre silently rejected the moral aim of comedy, while Farquhar accepted at least in theory that "Comedy is no more at present than a well-framed Tale handsomely told, as an agreeable vehicle for Counsel or Reproof."[34]

The Preface to *Love's Contrivance* also reflects the influence of Jeremy Collier: "tho' I did not observe the Rules of Drama, I took peculiar Care to dress my Thoughts in such a modest Stile, that it might not give Offence to any." Collier's *Short View of the Immorality and Profaneness of the English Stage* had been published in 1698. Centlivre had not at first been willing to accept Collier's arguments for the chastity of stage language. In the Preface to *The Perjured Husband* (1700), she had defended the language of the salacious subplot on the ground that it was not "reasonable to expect a person, whose Inclinations are always forming Projects to the dishonour of her Husband, shou'd deliver her Commands to her Confident in the Words of a Psalm." The reversal of position in the Preface to *Love's Contrivance* seems less a matter of personal conviction than a recognition of the changed expectations of the audience. For a very brief period in her career, Centlivre even accepted Collier's central contention that—as he announced at the opening of his *Short View*—"The Business of Plays is to recommend Virtue, and discountenance Vice."[35] In her Dedication to *The Gamester* (1705), Centlivre claimed that "The Design of this Piece were to divert, without that Vicious Strain which usually attends the Comick Muse, and according to the first intent of Plays, recommend Morality." Centlivre repeated the same ideas in the Dedication to her next play, *The Basset Table* (1705). This time she looked back to the ancient theaters as "Schools of Divinity and Morality" where comedy "laugh'd and diverted them out of their Vices; and by rediculing Folly, Intemperance, and Debauchery, gave them an Indignation for those Irregularities, and made them pursue the opposite Virtues." But after *The Basset Table*, Centlivre reverted to her original conviction, that the business of comedy was to entertain.

Centlivre's career spanned a period of great change in English comedy. Her first play appeared a few months after Congreve's *The Way of the World* (1700) and her last one only two months before Steele's *The Conscious Lovers* (1722). John Loftis has traced the influences on comedy of the social changes that took place over this period. He notes particularly Centlivre's response to "the new ethical thought . . . the Collier controversy and its aftermath . . . and the increased importance of merchants in English society."[36] The influence of ethical benevolism can be observed in *The Gamester* and in the "sentimental" parts of *Marplot* and *The Artifice*. The negative influence of Collier has been noted already; it can be seen more generally in Centlivre's more decorous attitude to sexual morality after *The Perjured Husband*. The rise of the status of merchants can be seen in Centlivre's increasingly sympathetic attitude toward them from Sir Toby Doubtful in *Love's Contrivance* to Frederick in *The Wonder*. Pat Rogers, indeed, has called Centlivre a "witty chronicler of the emerging merchantile society."[37] It is not easy to be sure how far Centlivre was responding to these changes from artistic conviction and how far she was simply following the prevailing currents. Perhaps the two were never actually at odds: since she believed that comedy should entertain, it would be natural for her to respond to whatever changes in public taste she observed. Her attitude to merchants would also have been influenced by her Whig belief in the virtue and utility of trade.

The main characters in Centlivre's comedies range from rich baronets to poor but deserving army officers: the principal women are mostly heiresses. Centlivre's plots lead to the marriage of usually two—rarely, one or three—pairs of lovers. These marriages combine love with economic security. These are the elements of what contemporaries called "genteel" comedy, a social rather than a literary description. But there are other, more characteristic, ingredients of Centlivre's comedies. Her strengths are well expressed in the Prologue that William Bond wrote for *The Artifice*:

> Ask not, in such a General Dearth, much Wit,
> If she your Taste in Plot, and Humour hit:
> Plot, Humour, Business, form the Comick Feast,
> Wit's but a higher-relish'd Sawce, at best;
> And where too much, like Spice, destroys the Taste.

Wit is certainly not an important element in Centlivre's plays. But "Plot, Humour, Business" is a good characterization of the main sources of her comedy. The typical Centlivre play is a skeletal plot based on love intrigues and is fleshed out with incidental humor and business.

In "Concerning Humour in Comedy" (1695) Congreve discriminated between humor, wit, and folly as comic effects; and between humor, habit, and affectation as their sources. He restricted "humor" to a "singular and unavoidable manner of doing, or saying any thing, Peculiar and Natural to one Man only; by which his Speech and Actions are distinguish'd from those of other Men."[38] Congreve explained the abundance and variety of humor in English comedy as the result of "the great Freedom, Privilege, and Liberty which the Common People of England enjoy."[39] Congreve's attitude to humor and eccentricity is more tolerant and sympathetic than Ben Jonson's earlier in the seventeenth century or than Pope's attitude to the "ruling passion" in the early eighteenth century. For Congreve, approval of humor was almost a patriotic question. Centlivre follows Congreve in this tolerant—and decidedly Whiggish—attitude to humor, but in her plays she allows herself a greater latitude than Congreve prescribed. In her comedies, humor may be the result of an oddity or peculiarity of temperament; but it may also derive from habit or affectation. Thus, Congreve himself would have excluded many of Centlivre's humor characters from his definition.

In *The Stolen Heiress*, Larich's humor is that he wants his daughter at all costs to marry a scholar. In *The Artifice*, Widow Headless wants her second husband to be a lord. In other respects, these characters are conventional portraits of the tyrannous father and the amorous widow. Thus, they are not humors as Congreve understood the term. In *A Bold Stroke for a Wife*, the only true humorist in Congreve's sense is Ann Lovely's deceased father: "the most whimsical, out-of-the-way tempered man I ever heard of."[40] His humor is the mainspring of the play's action. As a condition of inheriting her fortune, Anne must marry with the consent of her four ill-assorted guardians: a beau, an antiquary, a stockjobber, and a Quaker. The guardians are really occupational types, but Centlivre treats them as humors. Again, they are not singular enough to come within Congreve's strict application of the term.

Nominally at least, comedy was supposed to correct humors. Farquhar claimed that "we have the most unaccountable Medley of Humours among us of any People upon earth; these Humours produce variety of Follies . . . these new Distempers must have new Remedies, which are nothing but new Counsels and Instructions."[41] Thus the character of Periwinkle in *A Bold Stroke for a Wife* could be regarded as a satirical attack on false and excessive antiquarianism. But more likely he was enjoyed for the comedy he provided: in actual practice, dramatists were content to exhibit humors without worrying too much about correcting them. As the eighteenth century progressed, humors were increasingly enjoyed and even approved for their own sake. Centlivre's Marplot is an early example of the "amiable humorist."[42]

Comic business is stage action as opposed to dialogue. Because business plays a more prominent part in comedy and farce than in serious plays, the word has tended to acquire a pejorative meaning. But for Centlivre and her contemporaries, business was an integral part of comedy. She regularly provided opportunities for business to give the actors outlets for their talents and to amuse the audience. Such business could descent to mere buffoonery, as it does in *The Man's Bewitched*. Laura is affecting madness, and sings: "Give me Liberty and Love. Give me Love and Liberty—Come, why don't you sing," she asks Sir David, while "She beats time all this while, with her hand upon his head, and with her foot upon his toes."[43] A good piece of business—a good stage joke, at least—is Jeffrey's bringing in the clogs on a plate in *The Artifice*.[44]

Centlivre's Preface to *The Perplexed Lovers* contains some interesting comments on business and humor. The actor-managers had differed about the comedy's effectiveness. Centlivre had reason to hope it would be successful "from Mr. Cyber's [i.e. Cibber] Approbation, whose Opinion was, that the Business wou'd support the Play; tho' Mr. Wilks seem'd to doubt it, and said, there was a great deal of Business, but not laughing Business; tho' indeed I cou'd not have dress'd this Plot with much more Humour, there being four Acts in the Dark." Centlivre's point is that the Spanish plot, most of which takes place after dark, prevented the display of much humor, and she had therefore to depend more on business. Centlivre relied instead on a whole series of mistaken identities in the dark. Wilks and Cibber disagreed about how amusing this would be. The play's failure would appear to have vindicated Wilks's opinion. Throughout this study, humor and business are used with the meanings discussed here.

VI *Pope and the "Cook's Wife"*

A short account of Centlivre's relations with her greatest contemporary makes a fitting conclusion to an introduction to her life and writings. She was obnoxious to Pope on several counts. She wrote for a living while Pope saw writers who pandered to popular taste in order to earn their bread as a threat to literature. She was a Whig in politics and violently anti-Catholic in religion, while Pope was a Tory and a Catholic. In 1714, the association of Centlivre with hireling scribblers and party hacks was confirmed, for Pope, by a suggestive coincidence. In April of that year, Edmund Curll published his first attack on Pope—a pamphlet by Charles Gildon—and his first piracy of a Pope poem.[45] In May Curll published Centlivre's new play *The Wonder*, with its outspokenly Whig Dedication to the Duke of Cambridge. Thus politics, literature, and religion all contributed to fix Centlivre, in Pope's mind, as a dunce.

Pope's dislike of Centlivre was intensified in March 1716 after the publication of *The Catholic Poet: or, Protestant Barnaby's Sorrowful Lamentation*.[46] This attack on Pope and his translation of Homer was probably the work of John Oldmixon, but Pope thought Centlivre had at least a share in it. He therefore included her among the Curll hacks that he pilloried in *A Full and True Account of a Horrid and Barbarous Revenge by Poison on the Body of Mr. Edmund Curll* and its sequel, *A Further Account* (both 1716).[47] In the second pamphlet, he has Curll send for his hireling authors to plan their revenge on Pope. Among them is Centlivre, referred to not by name but as "the Cook's Wife in Buckingham Court," where the Centlivres had lived since 1713. Among the resolutions made by the assembled hacks is one that "a Ballad be made against Mr. Pope, and that Mr. Oldmixon, Mr. Gildon and Mrs. Centlivre do prepare and bring in the same."[48]

In January 1717, *Three Hours after Marriage*—a farce by Gay, Pope, and Arbuthnot— was produced at Drury Lane. One of the characters in the play is Phoebe Clinket, a female dramatist who experiences difficulty in getting her new tragedy accepted for the theater. Commentators have disagreed about whether Phoebe Clinket is intended to satirize Centlivre, or the amateur poetess Lady Winchelsea.[49] Despite the evidence that some contemporaries thought that Clinket was intended for Lady Winchelsea, Centlivre is the more plausible victim. Lady Winchelsea never wrote for the public stage, whereas Centlivre always did, and often had difficulties getting her plays produced. *Three Hours after Marriage* is also, in part, a parody of Centlivre's favorite comedy of intrigue, with its plots, disguises, and frequent exits and entrances. Centlivre retaliated with a dig at Pope and *Three Hours after Marriage* in *A Bold Stroke for a Wife*.[50]

Pope subsequently included Centlivre in *The Dunciad* (1728). In the annotated version, *The Dunciad Variorum* (1729), the reason for her inclusion is given: "She also writ a Ballad against Mr. Pope's Homer before he begun it." This is evidently *The Catholic Poet*; in the appendix that lists attacks on Pope it is ascribed to "Mrs. Centlivre and others."[51] Later still, Pope linked Centlivre with Aphra Behn, Mary Manley, and Eliza Heywood as "fower remarkable poetesses & scribblers. . . . Ladies famous indeed in their generation."[52] All four were professional women of letters. For Pope, their existence, and still more their successes, were alarming evidence of the breakdown of traditional cultural values and of the decline of public taste. In Centlivre's case, his disapproval of the writer was sharpened by his dislike of the political and religious opinions of the woman.

CHAPTER 2

Writing to Please the Town

CENTLIVRE was a pragmatic dramatist: not for her Ben Jonson's defiant "By—'tis good, and if you lik't, you may."[1] Instead, she would have agreed with Samuel Johnson that "The drama's laws the drama's patrons give,/For we that live to please, must please to live."[2] In the Preface to *Love's Contrivance*, Centlivre recognized that "Writing is a kind of Lottery in this fickle Age, and Dependence on the Stage as precarious as the Cast of a Die; the Chance may turn up, and a Man may write to please the Town, but 'tis uncertain, since we see our best Authors sometimes fail." The public capriciousness is expressed more graphically in the Prologue to the same play: "Poets like Mushrooms rise and fall of late." The audiences of Centlivre's day were less homogeneous than they had been, and it was increasingly difficult to predict what would be popular.

Centlivre's first four plays were her apprenticeship in this uncertain art of writing to please the town. She experimented with tragedy, "genteel" comedy, romantic comedy, and farce. Only the last of the four, *Love's Contrivance*, was a success. In the search for the elusive formula that would hit the public taste, Centlivre also experimented with mixed genres. The Prologue to *Love's Contrivance* describes the play as "A hodge podge Dish serv'd up in China Ware," the dramatic equivalent of the "fam'd Ragoust" and "new invented Salate" that were currently in vogue at the most fashionable eating houses. But mixing genres can create new problems. A recurrent failure in these early plays is Centlivre's inability to forge the separate elements into a coherent whole. This problem recurs throughout Centlivre's dramatic career. Her last play is even more of a "hodge podge Dish" than her first. Some of her plays do achieve a satisfying unity, but in others she seems not to have considered it an important effect. She preferred variety and contrast, even at the cost of incongruity.

These four early plays must be judged as the experiments they were. They show us an inexperienced dramatist gradually working

31

toward the kind of play that would satisfy both her artistic conscience
and her desire for popular success. A second round of experiments
would be needed before she achieved this aim with *The Busy Body* in
1709.

I   The Perjured Husband *(1700)*

Centlivre's first play, *The Perjured Husband: or, the Adventures of
Venice,* was completed by March 1700. In a letter of that month, Abel
Boyer wrote her that "Mr. B— has perus'd your Play, and thinks the
Catastrophe too abrupt."[3] It was produced at Drury Lane in the fall.
The date of the first performance is not known, but it was published
on October 22. According to the Preface, it "went off with general
Applause" and only the lack of "good Actors and a full Town"
prevented it reaching a sixth night. But this general approval had not
been unanimous. Some critics had been "pleas'd to carp at one or two
Expressions" used in the subplot. Centlivre makes a spirited defense
of these "Expressions" as being suitable to the characters who spoke
them. She insists that the stage only reflects life and suggests that the
reformers should turn their attention to the manners and morals of
the town itself. When the town itself is reformed, the stage will follow
its example.

The Perjured Husband is technically original but morally derivative. The main plot is in the tradition of the "love and honor" tragedy,
and the subplot is a variant on the cuckolding intrigue characteristic
of restoration comedy. The play is set in Venice at carnival time: the
season when women enjoy greater license than during the rest of the
year. This setting is important only in the subplot, where the carnival
atmosphere is reminiscent of that in Aphra Behn's *The Rover* (1677).
During the carnival, intrigue is endemic, and disguise and
deception—convenient for the comic dramatist—are the order of the
day. The tragic plot is only nominally localized: it could take place
anywhere.

The tragic action is a story of entangled love. Bassino has come to
Venice on a diplomatic mission from his native Turin, where he has
left his wife Placentia. In Venice, however, he has fallen in love with
Aurelia. She returns his love, despite her previous betrothal to
Alonzo. Bassino conceals the fact that he is already married and plans
a bigamous marriage with Aurelia. Bassino has a faithful friend,
Armando, who tries to persuade him to give up Aurelia and return to

Placentia. Thus the dramatic situation is similar to Dryden's *All for Love* (1677), although it is worked out on a smaller social and emotional scale. Bassino, like Antony, is torn between love (Aurelia, his Cleopatra) and honor (Placentia, his Octavia). The faithful friend (Armando, his Ventidius) urges the claims of honor. But the parallel between the two plays does not extend beyond this skeleton of situation. Centlivre has none of Dryden's emotional or rhetorical powers. Her characters conduct low key arguments about the rival claims of love and duty. The characterization is too weak and colorless for us to take much interest in their decisions; and the rivals are not sufficiently contrasted. The confrontation between Aurelia and Placentia is a mere whisper in comparison with the great battles of words in *All for Love* and in Nathaniel Lee's *The Rival Queens* (also 1677).[4] Yet it seems likely that Centlivre was inspired to write tragedy by her great predecessor Dryden: in a letter written shortly after his death in 1700 she says how much she admired his works.[5] It would be natural for such admiration to be translated into imitation, before she discovered that her own dramatic gifts lay in quite another direction.

The catastrophe of the tragic plot is brought about—too abruptly, as the acute "Mr. B—" noticed—when Placentia, having failed to persuade Aurelia to renounce Bassino, stabs and kills her. Bassino enters at the very instant, and stabs Placentia before realizing who she is. Alonzo enters and revenges himself for the loss of his love by stabbing Bassino. These mistakes are cleared up, and the enemies forgive each other before they die. Alonzo and Armando are left to mourn the dead. The effectiveness of the scene—and it is the climax of the play—is impaired by the excessive length to which the business of dying is prolonged. The scene is a thick sandwich of talk with a thin filling of action in the middle, where the stabbings occur. Having brought on the catastrophe too suddenly, Centlivre prolongs it unskillfully. A better modulation of pace and tension would have made the ending more acceptable: as it is, it is difficult not to laugh. Lessing recognized this defect when he adapted part of the play for his *Miss Sara Sampson* (1755). He replaced the dagger with poison and put the incident in the penultimate act.[6]

The tragic parts of *The Perjured Husband* are written in a blank verse that is loose in metre but stiff in style. Sometimes it is only the lineation that reminds us that we are reading verse. Much more successful is the vigorously colloquial prose of the subplot. A notable example is the brief scene (p. 20) in which Ludovico reviews his schedule of intrigues. In a few lines, Ludovico is endowed with a vitality which the tragic characters never acquire.

The vigor of the subplot extends beyond its language. It centers on the Pizalto household, which comprises an old but lecherous husband (Pizalto), his young and amorous wife (Lady Pizalta), and her resourceful maid (Lucy). The Pizaltos are tired of each other. Ludovico is a Frenchman visiting Venice. Lady Pizalta sees him at a masquerade, is attracted, and employs Lucy to make a series of assignations that culminates in the cuckolding of her husband. If Pizalto is wronged, he is himself unfaithful. He intrigues with Lucy, but she outwits him. She first puts a very high price on her favor and then contrives to get Pizalto's money without granting it. Ludovico gains access to Lady Pizalta disguised as Lucy, but he is unluckily discovered by Pizalto on his way out. Pizalto's amorous designs soon result in the detection of the imposture. Ludovico's narrow escape leads him to resolve to "leave the wenching trade" and take a wife. Lucy offers herself at the opportune moment, armed with the fortune that she has just extorted from Pizalto. But Ludovico, although he admires her wit and relishes her money, refuses to consider marrying a chambermaid.

This subplot contains the embryo of future Centlivre comedies. The scene in which Ludovico is discovered by Pizalto (p. 31) is the prototype of a whole series of similar incidents. In future, though, the young man will generally be courting the woman he wants to marry, not engaged on a cuckolding intrigue. Lucy is the forerunner of a whole line of resourceful and mercenary chambermaids.

It may seem incongruous that Centlivre should combine two such different plots in one play, but it was in accord with contemporary practice. When Charles Johnson's tragicomedy *The Force of Love* (1710) was unsuccessful, he separated the serious and comic plots and presented them as two plays.[7] The two actions in *The Perjured Husband* are so distinct that Centlivre could well have done the same. There are two scenes—the masquerade scenes at the beginning of Acts I and V—where characters from both plots are on stage at the same time, although they do not speak to each other. Apart from these occasions, the two plots are kept entirely apart. Such was the common practice, but it did not always meet with critical approval. Neoclassical critics objected to tragicomedy as a hybrid form, and any kind of subplot offended against the rule of unity of action. This point of view is voiced by Lisideius in Dryden's critical dialogue *Of*

Dramatic Poesy (1668): "many scenes of our tragi-comedies carry on a design that is nothing of kin to the main plot . . . we see two distinct webs in a play, like those in ill wrought stuffs; and two actions, that is, two plays, carried on together, to the confounding of the audience; who, before they are warm in their concernments for one part, are diverted to another; and by that means espouse the interest of neither."[8]

Dryden himself did not accept this view. Through the character of Neander, he contrasts "the barrenness of the French plots" with "the variety and copiousness of the English." Neander defends the subplot through a suggestive metaphor. English plays, he says, "besides the main design, have under-plots or by-concernments of less considerable persons and intrigues, which are carried on with the motion of the main plot; just as they say the orb of the fixed stars, and those of the planets, though they have motions of their own, are whirled about by the motion of the *primum mobile* in which they are contained." This is a good image for *The Perjured Husband*. Although there is no causal link between the two plots, there is a strong thematic connection that acts like Dryden's *primum mobile*. This is the theme of fidelity and responsibility in love. In the main plot this theme is treated in heroic style, while in the subplot the same problem is examined from a comic viewpoint. Bassino and Ludovico both want sexual variety and gratification without responsibility. Ludovico's frank avowal of libertinism serves as an ironic comment on Bassino's high flown attempts to justify deserting his wife and deceiving his mistress. Ludovico punctures Bassino's posturings.

Unfortunately, the play fails to develop this potentially interesting contrast into serious social criticism. It fails because the main plot is disembodied and peopled with unreal characters. Where the subplot is exploratory and critical, with an appropriately open ending that leaves the problems unresolved, the tragic plot seems merely the working out of a lifeless formula. Centlivre's failure to resolve the subplot—Ludovico simply walks off stage after rejecting Lucy's offer—is an honest refusal to manufacture an answer to a difficult problem. By contrast, the multiple deaths and last minute repentances of the tragic plot strike an artificial note. Evidently Centlivre realized this herself, for subsequently she turned away from tragic modes. The experience of *The Perjured Husband* taught her that she could write comedy better and that it gave her greater opportunity to express what she wanted to say and to explore real social problems.

II   The Beau's Duel (1702)

If *The Perjured Husband* looks back to the restoration for its models and inspiration, *The Beau's Duel: or, A Soldier for the Ladies* is more obviously a product of its own time. Produced at Lincoln's Inn Fields in the late spring of 1702, it is set in contemporary London and reflects the mood of national optimism that greeted the outbreak of the War of the Spanish Succession. England had declared war on France and Spain in May, and at least one scene in *The Beau's Duel* was probably a late addition intended to capitalize on the new enthusiasm for the military. This is the recruiting scene.[9] But as the subtitle "A Soldier for the Ladies" indicates, the whole play reinforces the theme that "None but the Brave deserves the Fair." The Prologue promises the soldiers, "Let but your Arms abroad Successful prove, / The Fair at home shall Crown your Toyles with Love."

The play centers on a lively quartet of lovers. Colonel Manly is in love with Clarinda, and his friend Captain Bellmein is in love with her cousin Emilia. There is no "love chase" in the play, but there are several obstacles that have to be overcome before the happy pairs can be united in marriage. The first is a misunderstanding that arises from mistaken identities. The two men think they are in love with the same perfidious woman; and the two women suppose they are in love with the same double-dealing man. This mistake is rapidly cleared up. A more serious obstacle is Careful, Clarinda's father who wants her to marry the rich fop Sir William Mode. A third, less formidable, pretender to Clarinda is Ogle. Much of the play is taken up with exposing the folly and cowardice of Sir William and Ogle. The most important scenes are the mock-duels that give the play its name. In a tavern, Sir William and Ogle are tricked into fighting each other, rather in the way Olivia and Sir Andrew Aguecheek are in *Twelfth Night*. The two reluctant adversaries retire to Hyde Park, where—armed only with harmless foils—they pretend to fight it out. But this ruse is discovered by Clarinda and Emilia, who have disguised themselves as men. The humiliation of Sir William and Ogle is completed when they are insulted and kicked by the two women. The cowardice of the pretenders is strongly contrasted with the unquestioned courage of Manly and Bellmein.

But the exposure of Sir William as a coward is not in itself enough to overcome Careful's opposition to Manly. For this a more complicated plot is needed. Careful is tricked into a mock-marriage with Mrs. Plotwell, a former mistress of Bellmein's. Careful marries her under the impression that she is a Quaker and will make a frugal wife. In order to spite the disobedient Clarinda, he settles his estate on Mrs. Plotwell. After the ceremony, she drops her Quaker disguise and assumes a new role—that of a shrew. Careful is astonished and readily promises to restore Clarinda and Manly to favor if they can rid him of this wife. The deception is revealed. Careful forgives the trick, the four lovers are made happy, and even Sir William is philosophical about the loss of Clarinda. Only the despicable Ogle is excluded from the general reconciliation. The play is original, except for Mrs. Plotwell and the mock-marriage trick, which are taken from Jasper Mayne's *The City Match* (1639).

The four lovers in *The Beau's Duel* comprise a serious pair (Manly and Clarinda) and a lighter pair (Bellmein and Emilia). The contrast between the two pairs is effectively established in the first act, in separate scenes between the two men (pp. 2–5) and the two women (pp. 9–11). Such a pattern was more common after 1700 than it had been before. An early and influential example is Sir Richard Steele's *The Funeral* (1701).[10] The improved moral tone of *The Beau's Duel*—compared to the subplot of *The Perjured Husband*—is also indicative of the change that was taking place in comedy. In the opening scene, Bellmein's libertinism is contrasted with Manly's constancy in love. Mrs. Plotwell is actually one of Bellmein's cast-off mistresses. In Act IV he reflects, "If I had but got a Maidenhead, or made a Cuckold, it would not have vext me" (p. 38). But for all this, Bellmein has not overstepped the narrower liberties allowed to libertines in post-Collier comedy. Mrs. Plotwell assures us that "the awful Lustre of Virtue has always met with due respect" from him (p. 19). The seduction of an innocent woman would have excluded Bellmein from the reward of marriage to one of the heroines. Another example of the newer moral tone is that Clarinda and Emilia have scruples about the propriety of disguising themselves as men. Heroes and heroines are now more narrowly confined than their restoration counterparts; Smith has described what he calls the "disciplining" of the gay hero and heroine.[11] The typical protagonists are now men and women of sense, honesty, and discretion.

There are two groups of subsidiary characters in *The Beau's Duel*: the allies of the lovers (Mrs. Plotwell and Toper) and their adversaries (Careful, Sir William, and Ogle). Our response to them is controlled by the degree of sympathy with which Centlivre presents them. The most contemptible is Ogle, a former apprentice who has inherited money and independence. His humor is imagining that every

woman—even if he has never exchanged a word with her—is in love
with him. He conducts an "intrigue" with Clarinda on this basis:
Clarinda's maid keeps the letters and presents that he sends, and
Clarinda herself remains unaware of his existence. Sir William Mode,
a beau, is treated more mildly than Ogle. He is drawn after Sir
Novelty Fashion in Cibber's *Love's Last Shift* (1696). The inventive-
ness of his oaths—"blister me," "burn me," "impair my vigour"—is
amusing, but he is otherwise a pale imitation of Sir Novelty. Both he
and Ogle function primarily as foils to the military heroes. Careful is
nothing more than a conventional stage father who would rather his
daughter married a man of wealth than a man of sense.

Toper's humor is suggested by his name: he prefers the pleasures of
drinking to all others. The part was taken by George Powell,
notorious for his love of the bottle in real life. Toper is a functional
character: he is a useful extra in the duel scene and in the management of the intrigue with Mrs. Plotwell. But his part has the
additional interest of preserving evidence of a change in the author's
intentions. Toper's name was originally Roarwell. The evidence
occurs in signature E (pp. 25–32) of the first edition. At the end of Act
II, three speeches which obviously belong to Toper are assigned to
"Roarwell," and the tag at the end of the act puns on this name: "For
though we Roar . . ." (p. 25). At the beginning of Act III (p. 26),
Careful refers to Toper as "Roarwell." Neither name occurs in the
remainder of signature E; Roarwell appears nowhere else in the text.
His survival at all is probably due to careless proofreading.[12] The
evidence suggests that Toper was originally to have been a bully
instead of a drinker. Perhaps Centlivre after the outbreak of the war
made the change in order not to blur the contrast between fop and
soldier.

The part of Mrs. Plotwell, although borrowed from Jasper Mayne's
The City Match, is transformed by its new context in *The Beau's
Duel.* In *The City Match* the mock-marriage is part of a citizen-gulling
intrigue that reflects the antagonism between court and city that is
one of Mayne's major themes. This antagonism has no place in *The
Beau's Duel*: Careful, the victim of the trick, is not a merchant. In this
play, Centlivre is certainly not hostile to the city. Ogle boasts—
absurdly, since he is himself a former apprentice—of receiving a
letter "from a Merchants Wife, a City Animal, that pretends to a
nearer Taste than those of her Levell, and wou'd fain have a Child
with the Air of a Gentleman, but I beg'd her Pardon, I left her to the
Brutes of her own Corporation, for I will have nothing to do with the

Body Politick" (p. 16). The satire here cuts both ways: against the social pretensions of the city wife, but also against Ogle himself.

In one respect, the part of Mrs. Plotwell is decidedly ambiguous. In *The City Match* she was the wife of Young Plotwell. In *The Beau's Duel* she is Bellmein's former mistress. But a seasonable legacy has enabled her to regain her respectability: "Reputation is never lost but in an empty Pocket" (p. 20), as Bellmein comments. In the light of Mrs. Plotwell's dubious past, it seems a calculated equivocation when Centlivre gives her the final speech of the play: an encomium on "Virtue thou shining Jewel of my Sex" (p. 55). Whether this sentiment was taken seriously or not would be up to the audience. Those who wanted comedy to endorse morality could take it seriously; the more sceptical could remember Mrs. Plotwell's past and smile.

Altogether, *The Beau's Duel* is a very distinct advance on *The Perjured Husband*. Centlivre's social concerns, although not fully worked out, are given greater prominence. Comedy is brought to the center of the stage and made to reflect contemporary issues. Two scenes in particular are well handled: the double mistaken identity (pp. 36–38) and the scene after Careful has "married" Mrs. Plotwell (pp. 46–48). There are some loose ends: examples are the parts of Ogle and Toper and the recruiting scene. But for all this, *The Beau's Duel* can still be regarded as the first characteristic expression of Centlivre's art.

III   The Stolen Heiress *(1702)*

Centlivre's third play, *The Stolen Heiress:* or, *The Salamanca Doctor Outplotted,* was produced at Lincoln's Inn Fields on December 31, 1702. The original title was *The Heiress*: it was changed to *The Stolen Heiress* in the printed text, published on January 19, 1703. The change was evidently a late thought: the new title appears on the title page, the old one at the head of the text. Centlivre's—or rather Carroll's—authorship of her first two plays had been acknowledged. But with *The Stolen Heiress*, an attempt was made to conceal the author's name and sex. The Prologue begins "Our Author fearing his success to day, / Sends me to bribe your Spleen against his Play." The play was then published anonymously, and the use of pronouns in the dedication is studiously ambiguous. The idea of combatting prejudice against women as authors was not new. Mary Pix's *The Beau Defeated* (1700) appeared as a man's work. The Prologue speaks of the author as

"He" and the Dedication to the Duchess of Bolton is written in a strain of gallantry that was also intended to suggest male authorship. It is difficult to say how widespread such prejudice against women was, but it certainly existed. An extreme example is Critick in *A Comparison between the Two Stages* (1702): "What a Pox have the Women to do with the Muses? I grant you the Poets call the Nine Muses by the Names of Women, but why so? not because the Sex had any thing to do with Poetry, but because in that Sex they're much fitter for prostitution. . . . I hate these Petticoat-Authors."[13]

The Stolen Heiress is a tragicomedy set in Palermo, in a Sicily conceived of as remote and romantic rather than belonging to any particular period. It is a play about paternal tyranny, as socially disembodied as *The Perjured Husband* was. Gravello wants his daughter Lucasia to marry Count Pirro. Lucasia is in love with Palante, but Gravello prefers Pirro on account of his wealth. The rub is that Pirro is indifferent to beauty and attracted only by wealth. Gravello therefore gives out that his son Eugenio has died while on his travels. Lucasia thus becomes an heiress. Pirro swallows the bait and begins to negotiate with Gravello for Lucasia. In order to avoid the hated match, Lucasia runs away with Palante, and they are secretly married. Unfortunately, the treachery of Lucasia's maid leads Gravello to apprehend the lovers. He invokes the harsh Sicilian law that provides the death penalty for the theft of an heiress. Palante and his friend and accomplice Clerimont prepare to die heroically.

The situation is saved by Eugenio, who had returned to Palermo unexpectedly at the beginning of the play. Hearing the news of his own death, he prudently assumes an incognito. When he discovers his father's plan, he determines to thwart it. Still incognito, he reveals to Pirro that Eugenio is still alive. Pirro agrees to pay Eugenio for removing the inconvenient son and signs an agreement to that effect. Palante and Clarimont go on trial. At the critical moment, after pleas for mercy for them have failed, Eugenio drops his disguise and produces the incriminating agreement with Pirro. Palante and Clerimont are freed for Lucasia is no longer an heiress. The general rejoicing is augmented by the sudden and unexpected arrival from exile of Euphanes, a noble and wealthy lord. He reveals that Palante is not a foundling—as had been supposed—but his son. Gravello now cheerfully accepts him as a suitable son-in-law.

The main plot is thus serious in tone and potentially tragic. The subplot is a comic treatment of the same theme of parental tyranny. Larich is determined to marry his daughter Lavinia to a scholar. His choice has fallen on a foolish pedant, Sancho, the "Salamanca Doctor" of the subtitle. But Lavinia is in love with the more sensible and engaging Francisco. Together they outplot Larich and Sancho. The seasonable death of a rich uncle provides Francisco with a fortune. Larich is thereby reconciled to the match, and Sancho is resigned to the loss of Lavinia.

The Stolen Heiress was published with a Latin tag on the title page: "Nihil dictum quod non ante dictum." This is a rough paraphrase of a line from the Prologue to Terence's *Eunuch*. Just as Terence's play was an adaptation of Menander, *The Stolen Heiress* is a reworking of an earlier play: Thomas May's *The Heir* (1620). *The Heir* is a romantic comedy with strong affinities with Shakespeare and Fletcher. *The Stolen Heiress* is an interesting but imperfect attempt to reshape *The Heir* to suit the taste of 1701. Centlivre's revision was most successful in the subplot, which she makes into a vigorous comedy of intrigue. But this very success creates an incongruity between main plot and subplot. Romantic motifs such as the harsh law against lovers, the long-lost son, and Eugenio's incognito seem less at home than they were in *The Heir*. On the credit side, Centlivre made some sound structural and other improvements.

Centlivre connected the two actions of the play by making Gravello (May's Polimetes) and Larich (Franklin) brothers. *The Heir* is entirely in verse: Centlivre turned the subplot and the less emotional scenes of the main plot into prose. She is more flexible about the use of prose and verse than she had been in *The Perjured Husband*. Lucasia and Palante can drop into prose if appropriate, and the verse is thus reserved for serious or emotional scenes. The two plots are now neatly contrapuntal. Gravello's prejudice in favor of wealth appears no less absurd than Larich's superstitious reverence for pedantry. In *The Heir*, Franklin was simply a tyrannical father, and Shallow—his prospective son-in-law—what his name implies. Centlivre made them two humor characters. The subplot in *The Stolen Heiress* is consequently broader and more farcical than in *The Heir*. This is good in itself—but it makes the main plot appear lifeless by comparison. As in *The Perjured Husband*, the realistic treatment of the subplot makes us impatient with the artificial main plot.

Centlivre also speeded up the action of the play by omitting several of May's set piece scenes. A good example is the long satiric scene in Act IV in which May pillories the Catholic practice of selling absolution and exposes the quibbling habits of the legal profession.[14] Centlivre also omitted three scenes in which May was obviously imitating Shakespeare: the "love at first sight" episode that recalls *Romeo and Juliet*; the scene with the blundering watch that reminds us of Dogberry and Verges; and the offer of a pardon for a brother in exchange for his sister's chastity, which recalls *Measure for Measure*.[15] Centlivre omitted the "love at first sight" scene because she preferred intrigue to romance. As in most of her plays, she works with men and women who are already in love. The blundering watch was rejected in favor of a more complicated stratagem to reveal Pirro's plot—the signed bargain with Eugenio. Both omissions reflect Centlivre's dominant interest in the comedy of intrigue. The third omission, the scene that recalls Angelo, was probably left out in compliance with contemporary notions of propriety.

Centlivre's concern for decorum can also be seen in a minor but significant change she made to the plot. Luce in *The Heir* (Centlivre's Lavinia) appears on stage as if pregnant.[16] Throughout the play we naturally assume that she is; but in Act V May reveals that the supposed pregnancy was only a trick intended to alienate Shallow.[17] Centlivre suppresses the pregnancy. Only as a last and desperate stratagem to delay the match with Sancho does Lavinia pretend to be pregnant. We are told in an aside that this is a trick. Comtemporary audiences were sensitive to such matters. In Farquhar's *The Twin Rivals* (1702), the plot includes a character (Clelia) who is pregnant as a result of having been seduced: but she is not allowed to appear. When the play was published, Farquhar replied to critics who had objected to an important character remaining offstage. He explained in the Preface that he "had rather they should find this Fault, than I forfeit my Regard to the Fair, by showing a Lady of Figure under a Misfortune."[18]

IV Love's Contrivance (1703)

Love's Contrivance: or, Le Médecin malgré lui was produced at Drury Lane on June 4, 1703. Its initial run of three nights was modest enough: but a truer measure of its popular appeal is that it enjoyed occasional revivals until 1726. The anonymity that began with *The Stolen Heiress* was continued. When the play was published on June 14, the Dedication was signed with the initials "R. M." On June 16, an advertisement was inserted in the *Daily Courant* denying that these were the author's real initials and promising shortly to reveal the "true name." No subsequent announcement has been traced, but Centlivre acknowledged her authorship of the play in the Dedication to *The Platonic Lady* (1706). There she tells us that "passing for a Man's," *Love's Contrivance* enjoyed great success. The Preface to *Love's Contrivance* is one of Centlivre's most important critical statements. It expresses her belief that the primary function of comedy is to entertain.

As the subtitle indicates, *Love's Contrivance* is partly based on Molière. Centlivre used not only *Le Médecin malgré lui* (1666) but also *Le Mariage forcé* (1664) and *Sganarelle* (1660). In her Preface, she claimed that the borrowed scenes had "not suffer'd in the Translation." It is impossible to agree with this complacent verdict, but it must be remembered that Centlivre was writing for a coarser audience than Molière's. Centlivre recognized this in the Preface when she wrote that the "French have that light Airiness in their Temper, that the least Glimps of Wit sets them a laughing, when 'twou'd not make us so much as smile."

Perhaps because she was using three plays instead of one, Centlivre was more successful in imposing her own stamp on *Love's Contrivance* than she had been with *The Stolen Heiress*. A good indication of this success is that, for all her debt to Molière, there are closer similarities—in plot, character, and comic formula—between *Love's Contrivance* and her own *The Beau's Duel*. She borrowed particular scenes from Molière, but fitted them into her own comic framework. Both plays center on the outwitting of a tyrannous father. In *Love's Contrivance*, Selfwill (who corresponds to Careful in *The Beau's Duel*) has a daughter Lucinda (Clarinda) and her cousin Belliza (Emilia) living with him. Selfwill had previously agreed to a match between Lucinda and Bellmie (Manly); but mercenary considerations have induced him to reject Bellmie in favor of Sir Toby Doubtful (Sir William Mode). Bellmie is assisted in his intrigue by his friend Octavio (Bellmein). Octavio is a rakish contrast to the serious Bellmie; he pairs off with Belliza. There are naturally differences between the two plays. Instead of a beau (Sir William Mode), Centlivre uses an old city knight (Sir Toby Doubtful) as a comic butt. Instead of the mock-duels of the earlier play, broad farce is provided by scenes borrowed from Molière.

An unusual feature of *Love's Contrivance* that distinguishes it from *The Beau's Duel* and indeed from most of Centlivre's plays is the "love chase" between Octavio and Belliza. The couple meet for the first time in Act II, and she does not agree to marry him until the very end of the play. The scene in which they meet is an extended duel of wit quite untypical of Centlivre; it is one of the play's best scenes.[19]

Unfortunately, Centlivre chose not to develop this "gay couple" antagonism in the rest of the play. Attention is focused instead on the deception of Selfwill and Sir Toby and on Martin and his tricks. These are the parts of the play that she borrowed from Molière.

Centlivre tells us in the Preface that she originally planned a farce in three acts and that on the advice of friends she turned the play into a five act comedy. The skeleton of the original three act structure can still be discerned in the sequence of the three major farcical episodes: Martin's wife beating and Octavio's unwelcome interruption of it (pp. 10–13); Martin himself being beaten into admitting that he is a doctor (pp. 37–41); and the two fortunetelling scenes (pp. 53–58, 61–64). All these are based on Molière. The first two come from Le Médecin malgré lui (I, i–ii and iv), and the fortunetelling scenes from Le Mariage forcé (Scenes iv and v). Thus the original design of the play was evidently closer to Molière than the final version. As she revised, Centlivre added more of her own kind of comedy.

The character that is most Centlivre's own is Sir Toby Doubtful. His role corresponds to that of Sganarelle in Le Mariage forcé; but Molière's character is not a "city" figure at all. Sir Toby—old, lecherous, and miserly—seems at first to be a variant of the restoration stereotype of the merchant fit only to be cuckolded. But John Loftis points out that "there is no suggestion of social rivalry between merchant and gentleman" and that Sir Toby is rejected "because of his personal qualifications and his age rather than his social status."[20] In one scene, Sir Toby is actually a mouthpiece for the author's own sentiments. One of Lucinda's stratagems to dissuade Sir Toby from wanting to marry her is to make a series of extravagant demands that she hopes will horrify his city frugality. Dorimène makes extravagant demands in Le Mariage forcé (Scene ii). But Centlivre converts Dorimène's single long speech into a variant of the familiar "proviso scene" in which demands are made and answered item by item. Lucinda asks for a house in the fashionable district near St. James's; a new laced livery for her servants; a French coach and six horses to pull it; and she makes other demands calculated to shock not only Sir Toby's parsimony but his patriotism. The French coach is his particular aversion: "egad I wou'd not have a Nail about my Coach that's French, for the Wealth of the East-India Company. French Chariot! say ye, Zouns, Madam, do ye take me for a Jacobite?" (p. 48). This is a skillfully contrived scene. Because Lucinda is only pretending to make these demands, we do not suspect her of really being either frivolous or a Jacobite. At the same time, Sir Toby's impeccable

Whig reaction counts in his favor against his amorous folly in wanting to marry a young wife. Centlivre herself is able to express her favorite anti-French sentiments without stopping or even slowing the play in the process.

The other characters in *Love's Contrivance* correspond more closely than Sir Toby to their counterparts in *The Beau's Duel*. Bellmie is a serious and faithful lover like Manly. He is even shocked when Octavio assumes that he keeps a mistress (p. 22). Octavio takes after the more libertine Bellmein. He settles down to the idea of marriage to Belliza, but not without some pangs for the loss of his liberty (p. 25). There is a parallel contrast between the steady Lucinda and the flighty Belliza. There is with these two plays almost a sense of the dramatist "working it out like a sum on the blackboard," as F. W. Bateson puts it.[21]

Reviewing the four plays discussed in this chapter, one finds it natural to dismiss *The Perjured Husband* and *The Stolen Heiress* as false starts in genres not congenial to Centlivre's artistic bent. *The Beau's Duel* and *Love's Contrivance* are the plays that show the direction she was to take. But if *Love's Contrivance* marked the end of Centlivre's apprenticeship, she remained willing to experiment with new modes and genres. Her next play—*The Gamester* (1705)—was to be a complete break with the practice of *Love's Contrivance* and with the critical ideas expressed in its Preface.

CHAPTER 3

The Gamester
and Other Plays

I think the main design of Comedy is to make us laugh," Centlivre wrote in 1700; "if the Poet can be so happy as to divert our Spleen, 'tis but just he should be commended for it."[1] But in the early eighteenth century, a more serious comedy was emerging. In December 1703, Steele's decidedly "moral" play *The Lying Lover* was produced at Drury Lane. In January 1704, Queen Anne issued two proclamations for the better regulation of the stage. One ordered that "no play, new or old, no song, prologue or epilogue be presented on the stage without being first licensed by the Master of the Revels." The second ordered the Master of the Revels to be "careful in the perusing and licensing of plays."[2] In the Preface to *The Lying Lover*, Steele described it as his "honest Ambition to attempt a Comedy, which might be no improper Entertainment in a Christian Commonwealth." Referring to the recent royal proclamations, he expressed the hope that "by being encourag'd in the Interests of Virtue" comedy would "strip Vice of the gay Habit in which it has too long appear'd."[3]

The following season, two "moral" comedies were produced that were much more successful with the public than *The Lying Lover* had been. Both plays combined social comedy with the reformation of an erring character. Cibber's *The Careless Husband* was produced at Drury Lane in December 1704; Centlivre's *The Gamester*, at Lincoln's Inn Fields in January 1705. Thus, the phase of Centlivre's career that is charted in this chapter begins with a decisive break from her earlier theory and practice of comedy. But *The Gamester* is not a characteristic Centlivre play. Despite its success, she began in her next play to return to more congenial kinds of comedy. *The Basset Table* (1705) is nominally a "moral" play, but in it the earnestness of *The Gamester* is much diluted. Her next two plays—*Love at a*

Venture (1706) and *The Platonic Lady* (1707)—reject the idea of moral comedy entirely and return to the earlier model of *The Beau's Duel*.

I The Gamester *(1705)*

When Steele wrote *The Lying Lover*, his intention was "to write a Comedy in the Severity [Collier] required."[4] Steele based his play on Pierre Corneille's *Le Menteur* (1642). He added a good deal of comedy to the first four acts, but he made Act V entirely serious in tone. Kenny calls it "a highly emotional condemnation of duelling."[5] The result is an extreme and unsatisfactory contrast between the two parts of the play. Centlivre was partly following Steele's example when she turned Jean-Francois Regnard's *Le Joueur* (1696) into *The Gamester*. Like Steele, she was intent on writing a moral play. Her most significant alteration was also in the last act, where she introduced a happy or "sentimental" ending. But she profited from Steele's example and avoided too complete a separation of the serious from the comic. In the Dedication, she wrote: "The Design of this Piece were to divert, without that Vicious Strain which usually attends the Comick Muse, and according to the first intent of Plays, recommend Morality." *The Gamester* was an immediate and continuing success. The date of the first performance is not recorded, but it was published "as it is this Day acted the twelfth time" on February 22, 1705.[6] It was regularly revived for many years and was given occasional performances as late as 1756.

The main plot of *The Gamester* centers on the relationship between Valere and Angelica. They have long been in love, but Valere is a compulsive gambler, and Angelica has made it a condition of marriage that he forswear gambling. Valere has often promised to do so, but has always broken his word. When the play opens, his fortunes are at a low ebb. His father, Sir Thomas Valere, refuses to pay any more of his debts unless he marries Angelica. As a result, Valere begs her forgiveness once again, and she takes him back into favor. She gives him a diamond-studded miniature of herself and charges him to keep it on pain of losing her love. But after Valere has left Angelica, her power over him weakens. He breaks his promise not to gamble. In a long gaming scene, he first loses and then recoups his losses. Angelica is told what has happened. She disguises herself as a man and goes to where Valere is playing dice. She plays with him, and his good fortune deserts him. He loses all his money and she persuades him to stake the diamond-studded miniature. He loses it to her, and she leaves without revealing her identity. As soon as she is gone, Valere is affected by remorse. He makes a personal vow never to gamble again. This takes us to the end of Act IV.

The subplot deals with Angelica's widowed sister, Lady Wealthy. Her character is that of a "coquette-prude."[7] She trifles with her faithful lover Lovewell: never absolutely refusing him, while at the same time conducting mild flirtations to make him jealous. Lady Wealthy accepts the attentions of the Marquis of Hazard, an absurd frenchified fop. She is also attracted to Valere out of pure spite to Angelica. Lady Wealthy's compulsive coquettishness parallels Valere's compulsive gambling: both are vices that the play aims to cure. The two actions are linked when Lady Wealthy sends Valere a present of money. But Valere is Lovewell's friend and tells him about it. This action improves our idea of Valere's character. More importantly, it allows Lovewell to upbraid Lady Wealthy with her folly so generously and tactfully that she repents her coquetry and agrees to marry him. This reconciliation takes place at the beginning of Act V.

We return for a final climactic scene to the main action. Valere has come to see Angelica. She asks to see the miniature and naturally he cannot produce it. At first Valere tries to brazen it out, but he is crushed when Angelica produces it herself. He becomes penitent and submissive. At this point, Sir Thomas arrives. Hearing what has happened, he disinherits Valere. Angelica is shocked by this harshness: it makes her reflect on her own. She resolves to forgive Valere. Sir Thomas repents his hasty words and does the same. Valere and Angelica are at last united. All that remains is the exposure of the Marquis of Hazard: he turns out to be a footman who has assumed the alias in order to trap some woman of fortune. Four other characters have important subordinate roles. They are Dorante, Valere's uncle and rival for Angelica; Hector, Valere's resourceful servant; Mrs. Favourite, Angelica's maid; and Mrs. Security. The last is a pawnbroker and moneylender; she helps to set the tone of Valere's social world and is instrumental in the exposure of the sham Marquis.

Most of *The Gamester* is translated from *Le Joueur*. But Centlivre made some important alterations. In Regnard, La Comtesse is a minor figure. Centlivre expanded her part and added that of Lovewell to comprise a distinct subplot. Lady Wealthy is treated more sympathetically than Regnard's Comtesse. Centlivre also changed the ending of the play. In *Le Joueur*, Valère loses Angélique to Dorante. The play ends on a low key note, with Valère still devoted to gambling and hoping for better luck in the future. In order to prepare for her ending, Centlivre makes Valere more attractive and Dorante less sympathetic. In *The Gamester*, Dorante is an older man, and Centlivre insinuates that his interest in Angelica is financial . In *Le Joueur*, Valère pawns the miniature of Angélique almost as soon as he receives it. In *The Gamester*, Valere loses the picture only much later in the play and in circumstances that admit of some extenuation. Actually, Regnard's play is probably a more effective antigaming piece than Centlivre's. Valère is shown in *Le Joueur* as indifferent to all other pleasures and as degraded by his obsession. Centlivre does not show the evil consequences of Valere's gambling, for she lets him have his cake and eat it too. But her ending was in keeping with contemporary ideas of how a "moral" comedy should work. A happy ending and the reclamation of the erring hero were expected. *The Gamester* is like *The Lying Lover* and *The Careless Husband* in these respects.

Force of example is supposed to operate on the characters in the play just as the play itself is supposed to act on its audience. The selfless way in which Lovewell extricates Lady Wealthy from the awkward failure of her designs on Valere works an important change in her. "This generosity shocks me—" she admits in an aside.[8] It shocks her into repentance and reformation. Angelica's response to Sir Thomas's disinheriting his son is the same: "this Usage shocks me" (p. 66). It shocks her into examining her own conduct again. When Angelica relents, so does Sir Thomas: "your Example is too good not to be follow'd" (p. 67). This is just how the audience is invited to respond to exemplary comedy. Watching generous actions should lead us to imitate them. The same process is at work in *The Careless Husband*. Sir Charles Easy is reformed by the example of his wife's tender and generous response to her discovery of his affair with her maid Edging.

A serious problem for the modern reader of these comedies is the credibility of the reformations. Some contemporaries also responded skeptically. In *Love's Last Shift* (1696), Cibber had reclaimed a roving husband through the example of his wife's fidelity. Vanbrugh wrote a sequel—*The Relapse* (1696)—in which the probable aftermath of the husband's reformation is explored. No one wrote a sequel to *The Gamester* in which Valere is tempted to take up gambling again: but some of the audience must have been skeptical of the sincerity of his conversion. Centlivre certainly anticipated such skepticism, for she actually incorporated it into the play. Valere's servant Hector voices the skeptical reaction. Sir Thomas's disinheriting Valere evokes two contrasting asides:

> *Hector.* So, there's all my Wages lost.—
> *Angelica.* Ha! this Usage shocks me. (P. 66)

The juxtaposition of these two responses allows the audience to identify with either. Indeed, throughout the play Hector's asides serve to undercut Valere's pretenses.

Critics have been much exercised by the question of whether *The Gamester* is a sentimental play and, indeed, by what constitutes a "sentimental" play. The term was not used by contemporaries. Ernest Bernbaum has described "Confidence in the goodness of average human nature" as "the mainspring of sentimentalism."[9] Bernbaum argues that only if we accept the fundamental goodness of Valere's character—as a corollary of the fundamental goodness of human nature generally—can the sincerity of Valere's conversion be accepted without reservation. For Bernbaum, this "benevolism" makes *The Gamester* a "sentimental" play. Arthur Sherbo, on the other hand, refuses to accept the label "sentimental." He points to antisentimental moments in the play—such as Lady Wealthy's parody of a Valere speech of contrition (p. 16)—and to what he calls the "large element of the purely comic."[10] But Lady Wealthy's parody comes early in the play, before Valere's reformation. And even scenes that seem primarily comic may contribute to the play's satire and morality. The scene with Mrs. Security (pp. 12–14); the wooing of Lady Wealthy by the sham Marquis (pp. 18–21); the scene in which Valere's creditors try to dun him (pp. 33–35); and the first gaming scene (pp. 44–53): all help to create a social context for the play's moral attitude to gambling. They serve to associate gambling with a disreputable social milieu. In any case, no contemporary comedy—however serious in intention—could dispense with scenes of this kind. Examples can be found in both *The Lying Lover* and *The Careless Husband*. *The Gamester* is clearly the same kind of play. This fact is of more critical importance than is exactly what constitutes a "sentimental" play.

II   The Basset Table *(1705)*

Centlivre failed to repeat the success of *The Gamester* with her second "moral" play, *The Basset Table*. Produced at Drury Lane on

November 20, 1705, it ran for only four nights and was never revived. Yet modern readers are likely to find it a more enjoyable comedy than *The Gamester*. There is less emphasis on the moral reformation, and there is more social comedy. But perhaps most interesting is the character of Valeria and the play's treatment of the "woman question."

The Basset Table has a more complicated plot than *The Gamester*. The serious half of the play centers on a quartet of lovers who roughly correspond to those in *The Gamester*. Lady Reveller is a coquette-prude like Lady Wealthy; Lord Worthy is a man of sense and principle like Lovewell. Lady Reveller must be cured of her frivolousness—such as keeping the basset table that gives the play its title—before she can marry Lord Worthy. The second pair is similar, but roles and characters are reversed. Lady Lucy is serious and sententious; Sir James Courtly is the one who needs to be reformed.

There are two subsidiary plots. One is closely linked to the fashionable follies that revolve around the basset table. Mrs. Sago, the wife of a shopkeeper in the city, has caught the fashionable rage for basset. It leads her to live beyond her husband's means and involves her in a dangerous intrigue with Sir James. In the general moral reformation at the end of the play, Mrs. Sago is made to renounce her social climbing and return to the kind of life her husband can afford. She does so somewhat reluctantly.[11]

The fourth plot is connected with the other actions only through Sir Richard Plainman. He is Lady Reveller's uncle and she lives in his house; he also has a daughter Valeria. Sir Richard wants her to marry a Captain Hearty of the navy; Valeria wants to marry Ensign Lovely of the army. This is the least "serious" part of the play. There is nothing moral about the way in which Lovely—abetted by Hearty—tricks Sir Richard out of his daughter. These scenes are much enlivened by Hearty's nautical bluntness and Valeria's character as an amateur of science.

In *The Gamester*, Centlivre left the motivation of Valere's final reformation deliberately vague. We were simply asked to accept that, this time, his contrition was genuine and his reformation permanent. In *The Basset Table*, Centlivre is more explicit. We are shown how the characters are regenerated. In one case it is a gradual process and in the other a sudden shock. Sir James likes Lady Lucy, but can hardly resolve whether he wants to settle down. He has a long and serious talk with her in which she half convinces him to give up his follies.[12] But when she leaves him, he still hankers after "your Merry little Coquetish Tits" (p. 49). Reflection, though, convinces him that

Lady Lucy is right. He helps Lord Worthy to reclaim Lady Reveller and presents himself again—equally reformed—to Lady Lucy.

What was a gradual process with Sir James is effected on Lady Reveller by a sudden shock. Sir James passes a purse of guineas to her at a crucial point in a basset game. He subsequently corners her and intimates that he did not give the money for nothing. When she asks him why he has such a poor opinion of her virtue, he replies: "Can a Lady that loves Play so passionately as you do—that takes as much Pains to draw Men in to lose their Money, as a Town Miss to their Destruction . . . can you, I say, boast of Innate Virtue?" (pp. 55–56). Sir James is intensifying his attack when—as arranged between them—Lord Worthy enters and "rescues" Lady Reveller. But Sir James's words, if not his actions, were in earnest, and Lady Reveller takes the point. She is shocked out of her folly and agrees to reform and marry Lord Worthy. Her newly acquired sense is at once tested by the revelation of the trick. She agrees that the end justified the means.

In *The Gamester*, the focus was on gambling as Valere's personal vice. *The Basset Table* develops particularly the social evils that are associated with it. There is a marked contrast between the opening scenes of the two plays. *The Gamester* began with Hector alone, sleepy and waiting for Valere's return from an all-night gambling session. Valere returns, alone and disconsolate. In this scene and throughout the play, the effect of Valere's gambling is to isolate him and ostracize him from society. It separates him from his father and from Angelica and forces him into the company of people like the sharper Cogdie and Mrs. Security. Valere must give up gambling in order to resume his proper social position. *The Basset Table* opens with a public scene. It is dawn in the hall of Lady Reveller's house. Half a dozen footmen are waiting drowsily for their ladies. The basset table is about to break up. Here the emphasis is on gambling as a social blight. Many characters are involved in it. It turns night into day and day into night. It brings people together but for the antisocial purpose of cheating each other.

In *The Gamester*, Valere celebrated the social leveling, from dukes down, that takes place around the gaming table (p. 36). *The Basset Table* illustrates the evils that this social mix occasions. As in *The Gamester* (pp. 50-56), there is an important gambling scene in *The Basset Table* (pp. 50-54). In the earlier play the first half of the scene—before the entry of the disguised Angelica—functioned primarily as local color and social background. In the scene in *The*

Basset Table the excitement is more intense. All the players are important characters in the play, and we observe each move with interest as we follow the undercurrents of personal feeling that eddy below the decorous surface. Mrs. Sago's losses, for example, make her increasingly suspicious of what "game" Sir James is playing with her.

A second important theme in *The Basset Table* is the question of the education of women. Valeria is described in the list of characters as a "Philosophical Girl." She has interests in both speculative and experimental science. She reads Descartes and Fontenelle and dissects fish and worms. This is not at all what Captain Hearty has in mind for his wife. He gladly resigns her to Ensign Lovely and even helps the lovers to outwit Sir Richard. Lovely disguises himself as a sailor. Coached by Hearty, he imitates the nautical argot so well that he convinces Sir Richard and receives his consent to marry Valeria.

Valeria herself has been taken as a satirical portrait of a kind of "new woman" and even as a caricature of the feminist Mary Astell.[13] But there is nothing in the play to suggest that Centlivre intended us to regard Valeria satirically. Lovely has a couple of irreverent asides about Valeria's science (p. 30), but they do not by any means make us skeptical about its genuineness. Her scientific interests have not prevented her from falling in love; nor has she anything in common with Mary Astell apart from the desire to found an academy for women. The emphasis in Mary Astell's educational writings is pietistic and literary, not scientific or experimental. Sir Nicholas Gimcrack in Thomas Shadwell's *The Virtuoso* (1676) is clearly intended to expose to ridicule the "science" that he professes. But Valeria's empirical procedures and skeptical attitude are in the true spirit of the Royal Society. Valeria is not a satirical portrait, but a tactful and attractive vindication of the educated woman.

Valeria is an exceptional figure. The women dramatists of the time of Behn and Centlivre rarely presented in their plays the type of "new woman" they themselves aspired to be. But in *The Basset Table*, the theme is not confined to Valeria. The contrast between Lady Reveller and Lady Lucy is an illustration of Mary Astell's contention that for many women "Ignorance and a narrow Education, lay the Foundation of Vice, and imitation and custom rear it up."[14] Lady Reveller is presented as a woman of sense but unimproved by any education; consequently, she is giddy and lacks moral principle. Lady Lucy, on the other hand, is a woman whose native good sense has been improved by thought and reading. Valeria too is educated without being pedantic or prudish. She dissects a worm with the same calm rationality that is reflected in her attitude to Lovely. Once she has told him that she loves him, she refuses to coquet or play games simply in order to conform to the female stereotype (pp. 29-30).

The "woman question" and the basset theme are closely linked in the play. The educated either see nothing attractive in the card game, or if they do play they know when to stop. Sir James is cool enough to be able to play for diversion: he even calculates exactly how much he will let the ladies win (p. 49). His gambling is morally vicious not in itself, but because of its harmful effects on the women he "plays" with. Lady Lucy simply sees no point in basset, nor is Valeria ever tempted to play. But Lady Reveller and Mrs. Sago are more vulnerable. Their play exposes them to the loss not only of purse but of reputation. Sir Richard Plainman expounds the theme of the "lady's last stake": "For she whose Shame no good Advice can wake,/When Money's wanting will her Virtue Stake" (p. 6). Both Lady Reveller and Mrs. Sago come close to this situation, but it is a background threat rather than a central theme in the play. Cibber explores the problem at greater length in *The Lady's Last Stake* (1707): he may have taken some hints from *The Basset Table*.

One final aspect of the play that deserves mention is its treatment of the city. Sir Richard Plainman is described in the list of characters as "Formerly a Citizen, but now lives in Covent-Garden, a great lover of a Soldier, and an Inveterate Enemy to the French." Sir Richard is a much more attractive portrait of the merchant than Sir Toby Doubtful in *Love's Contrivance*. Like Sir Toby, he expresses Centlivre's anti-French sentiments, but Sir Richard is Centlivre's spokesman on other issues too. His disapproval of Lady Reveller's basset, quoted above, is a case in point. He is even a domestic tyrant from patriotic motives: he wants Valeria to breed a family of heroes to resist the French in the next generation. This foible apart, he speaks with sober and exemplary sense. Contrasted with Sir Richard are the foolish Sagos. The contrast is in part financial: Sir Richard is a wealthy merchant, Sago a modest shopkeeper. Mrs. Sago's fashionable folly and social climbing are condemned all the more because she cannot afford them: they expose her to ridicule and her husband to bankruptcy. Sago himself is a satiric butt not because he is a shopkeeper but because he is weak and credulous. Centlivre's social point is that wealthy merchants can mix on terms of equality with the fashionable world; but the smaller mercantile fry will only make themselves ridiculous—if the consequences are not worse—by trying to emulate their betters.

III   Love at a Venture *(1706)*

The Basset Table was a halfway house between serious moral comedy and straightforward laughing comedy. In *Love at a Venture*, Centlivre returned completely to the earlier mode of *The Beau's Duel*, abandoning altogether the plot and purpose of reformation. *Love at a Venture* is an amusing and well-constructed comedy. But unfortunately, London audiences never had a chance to see it. Instead, it was performed, according to the title page, "By his Grace, the Duke of Grafton's Servants, at the New Theatre in Bath." According to Mottley, the play had been offered to Drury Lane, but rejected. Centlivre "afterwards carried it to Bath, and there it was performed, and she herself acted a Part in it."[15] Another source *The Laureat* (1740), gives a more circumstantial account of the play's rejection, attributing it to Cibber on the ground that "it is silly, and it is not ridiculous."[16] Silly or not, Cibber thought well enough of the play to steal from it in writing *The Double Gallant* (1707). In his *Apology* (1740), he says that this play was "made up of what little was tolerable, in two, or three others, that had no Success, and were laid aside, as so much Poetical Lumber."[17]

Love at a Venture is based on the adventures of the familiar quartet of lovers. Bellair is lively and rakish; his foil, Sir William Freelove—despite his name—is serious and constant in love. Beliza is witty and coquettish; Camilla quiet and subdued.[18] As in *The Basset Table*, the lovers are paired by contrast: Bellair is united with Camilla, Sir William with Beliza. When the play opens, Bellair has three identities and two intrigues on his hands. His father has arranged a marriage for him with Camilla: but Bellair knows only of the match, not the lady's identity. Independently, Bellair has saved Camilla from drowning and hopes to improve the acquaintance. With Camilla he goes under the name of Constant. His third identity is Colonel Revel. This alias serves for his intrigue with Beliza. His friend Sir William is in love with Beliza, but Bellair does not know this. A good deal of comedy is created by Bellair's difficulties in keeping up all three identities. Beliza and Camilla, awkwardly for him, are cousins and share the same lodgings. Bellair has to try to convince them that he is indeed two people. Act IV contains his most elaborate attempt to do so: the two women summon him at the same time under his two

aliases. Bellair uses a skillfully stage-managed series of contrivances
to convince at least Camilla that he is not a single double-dealing
rogue; Beliza remains skeptical.

Throughout the play Centlivre develops a qualitative difference
between Bellair's feelings for Camilla and for Beliza. The first are
serious, the second light-hearted. When Bellair and Camilla are
finally confronted with their fathers—Sir Thomas Bellair and
Positive—Bellair can happily accept the idea of marriage to Camilla.
Beliza is persuaded to accept the faithful Sir William. Bellair's love is
"at a venture" in two senses. It is the result of chance, through his
accidental and serviceable meeting with Camilla on the river.
Secondly, it is pursued at the hazard of his life and fortune: his life
when he saved her from drowning, his fortune when he risks his
father's displeasure in determining to marry—as he supposes—
against his father's wishes. The morality of the play is sound if not
explicit. Bellair's honorable ventures pay off handsomely. His less
honest ones—his intrigues with Beliza and Lady Cautious—are
frustrated.

The play centers on Bellair and his disguises, but there are several
subsidiary sources of comedy. Sir William lives with his brother-in-
law Sir Paul Cautious. Sir Paul is old, jealous, and hypochondriacal;
he also has a young and attractive wife. When Sir William allows
Bellair to use his rooms for one of his disguises, Bellair meets Lady
Cautious and—it follows, of course—starts an intrigue with her. His
attentions are welcome enough to Lady Cautious, but their successive assignations are frustrated. At the end of the play, Sir William
reconciles Sir Paul and his wife, persuading both to behave with more
consideration and sense. Sir William has an unsatisfactory part in the
play: Bellair is allowed to flirt with his sister and his intended wife,
while Sir William is kept on the sidelines. Inevitably he appears the
dull spokesman for seriousness and morality compared with the gay
and active Bellair.

An additional source of comedy, not very well integrated into the
plot, is the humor character Wou'dbe. He is the very epitome of the
imitator. His particular humor is a slavish aping of Sir William's
clothes. The ideas that are his own are distinguished by their silliness:
examples are his project for clockwork streets and his plan of
education.[19] At the end of the play, Bellair advises him to "leave off
this foolish Whim of Mimicking" and Wou'dbe is expelled (p. 62). The
comic servants Patch and Robin also deserve mention, particularly
for a brief but effective exchange at the end of the play (p. 63) in which

they do not quite resolve to marry. Centlivre uses the same joke at the end of *The Busy Body* and a variant of it at the end of *The Wonder*. Obviously, she is here guying the conventional pairing off of servants at the end of a comedy.

Centlivre took the main plot of *Love at a Venture*—Bellair's two intrigues—from Thomas Corneille's *Le Galand doublé* (1660).Corneille's play, in keeping with French practice, has no subplot. Don Fernand (Bellair) intrigues with both Léonor (Camilla) and Isabelle (Beliza). Fernand does not know that Léonor is his father's choice for him. Fernand has a friend, Don Juan (Sir William), who helps him to manage the intrigues, but Don Juan is not involved with Isabelle at all. Sir William is largely Centlivre's creation. She added the relationship between him and Beliza, as well as the subplot with Sir Paul and Lady Cautious and the character of Wou'dbe. Apart from these additions, Centlivre's most important change was in the characterization of Bellair. She naturalized him into the English tradition of the rake settling down to marriage by making him less sententious and more of an "Airy Spark" than his French counterpart. Bellair is perhaps Centlivre's liveliest rake: a worthy successor, in a more sober age, to Celadon and Dorimant.

The loss of Don Fernand's sententiousness was partly a result of the change from Corneille's couplets to Centlivre's prose. Centlivre is less interested in verbal wit than in stage action. She therefore eliminated much of the verbal sparring in which Corneille's characters indulge. She tends to move on more rapidly after the comic point has been made. An example of the process can be seen in the use she made of the following two speeches—from different scenes—of Don Fernand's valet Guzman:

> Bon, mais puisqu' à la fois deux ont l'heur de vous plaire,
> Et que la confrérie est un mal nécessaire,
> Prenez-les toutes deuz en qualité d'époux,
> L'une pour vos amis, l'autre sera pour vous. (I,i)
> . . . .
> Monsieur, si par hasard elle était fort pressée,
> Et qu'à vous en défaire on vous vît empêché,
> Pour vous faire plaisir je prendrais le marché. (I, vi)[20]

Centlivre removed these lines from the cut and thrust of their original contexts, and combined them into a single speech of Bellair's valet Robin: "Why, Sir, if the worst come to the worst—that they will both have you—why en'e marry them both, keep one for your self, and

t'other to entertain your Friends—or, if you please, Sir,—to do you a
Service, I don't care if I take one of 'em off your hands" (p. 26). Here
the jokes are effectively naturalized into Robin's idiom.

Centlivre had less need for characters like Corneille's Guzman and
the confidants Jacinte and Béatrix, since *Love at a Venture* contains
two fully developed subplots. Centlivre's Robin, Patch, and Flora are
consequently less prominent in *Love at a Venture* than their originals
in *Le Galand doublé*. A particular example of Centlivre's shortening
their roles can be seen in her treatment of Corneille's Act I, Scene iv.
This is the scene in which Fernand, baulked of the mistress, woos the
maid. In *Love at a Venture*, Bellair's corresponding flirtation with
Patch is much shorter (pp. 9-12).

Bellair's compulsive rakishness, exercised almost automatically on
any attractive woman he meets, may remind us of the heroes of
Dryden and Etherege. But it is not allowed to go beyond the limited
libertinism that we observed in Bellmein in *The Beau's duel*. In *The
Perjured Husband*, Lady Pizalta was allowed to cuckold her husband
and get away with it. In *Love at a Venture*, Centlivre's attitude to
adultery is much less sympathetic. Bellair is not allowed to cuckold
Sir Paul. At the end of the play, Lady Cautious is glad that her
virtue—no thanks to herself—is still intact: "What sure Disgrace
attends Unlawful Love; had I really fall'n, I now shou'd die with
shame . . . methinks I hate my self, for having, but in wish,
consented, and grow in love with Virtue" (p. 54). The moral is here
underscored more heavily than it is in the case of Bellair's settling
down. A double standard operates to make Lady Cautious seem more
guilty in accepting than Bellair in offering love. But if Centlivre
refuses to allow Lady Cautious to amuse herself on the side, neither
does she allow her to escape. Her treatment of the problem of a young
woman married to an old husband is more honest than Farquhar's in
The Beaux' Stratagem (1707). Farquhar—in flagrant disregard of
contemporary legal realities—simply dissolves the Sullens' marriage.[21] Centlivre rejects this easy way out and uses the miseries of
the Cautious marriage to reinforce the play's argument that marriage
must be based on love. But *Love at a Venture* is more comic than
moral: in the main plot, Centlivre cuts the knot rather than untying it
when Bellair and his father turn out to have chosen the same woman.

IV   The Platonic Lady (*1706*)

The Platonic Lady is another variant on what is by now a familiar
comic pattern: a main plot with two pairs of contrasting lovers and

subsidiary humor characters providing comedy of a broader kind. The play has the usual quartet of lovers: the rakish Belvil and the serious Sir Charles Richley; Lucinda the "platonic" coquette-prude and the quiet and retiring Isabella.[22] The gay spark gets the quiet woman, and the coquette is paired with the sententious hero. Thus far the play repeats the formula of *Love at a Venture*. But the two plays are not really very similar. Lucinda, the "platonic lady," is an unusual humor character. Isabella dons a series of disguises in order to win Belvil. Belvil for most of the play is in active pursuit of Lucinda.

Belvil is the most important character in the play, with more of a preplay history than most Centlivre characters. He is of unknown parentage, at least until the end of the play. Chancing one night to lodge with Sir Thomas Beaumont and his niece Lucinda, Belvil was instrumental in saving them from an attack by robbers. Since then he has been on the friendliest terms with them; but Sir Thomas has mysteriously made him promise not to marry Lucinda without his consent. Belvil nevertheless thinks he is in love with Lucinda and hopes eventually to win Sir Thomas's consent. Previous to his acquaintance with Lucinda, however, Belvil had met and fallen in love with an unknown woman (actually Isabella) in Paris. Isabella and Sir Charles Richley have been contracted to marry by their parents but they dislike each other. Sir Charles is in love with Lucinda; Isabella with Belvil. Obviously a good deal of exposition is necessary to get all this information fed to the audience. Centlivre manages it skillfully, giving it piece by piece rather than in solid blocks.

The action of the play comprises three interwoven strands. The first is centered on Lucinda, courted by both Belvil and Sir Charles. Despite her platonic pretenses, her preference for Belvil is clear— until it is revealed that he is her brother. She then finds that Sir Charles will make an excellent husband. The second action is centered on Isabella. Her promising attachment to Belvil in Paris was suspended by her sudden and unexpected recall home. At that time they lost track of each other, but Isabella has now found Belvil again. She devises various stratagems in an attempt to reawaken his interest in her: they serve to fill out the plot, but have no effect on Belvil until the discovery that Lucinda is his sister. Only then does his love for Isabella rekindle. The third action is centered on Mrs. Dowdy, a rich widow, the relict—as we later learn—of the steward of Lucinda's and Belvil's father. Acting on the advice of Sir Thomas, Belvil pays court to her, ostensibly as a prospective husband, actually to gain access to certain legal papers. Sir Thomas suspects that these papers will reveal that the late steward Dowdy had cheated Lucinda and Belvil of their rightful property. Mrs. Dowdy has come to town to find a second husband. Her fortune makes her attractive to Sharper, a man about town who lives by his wits. Sharper marries her, only to find the fortune lost to its rightful owners.

If *Love at a Venture* reminds us of restoration comedy, *The Platonic Lady* recalls the prerestoration Cavalier drama. Centlivre's knowledge of prerestoration drama is evident from her use of *The City Match* and *The Heir* in *The Beau's Duel* and *The Stolen Heiress*. But *The Platonic Lady* has general affinities with Cavalier drama rather than borrowings from particular plays. The most obvious affinity is in the "platonic" theme. Alfred Harbage has traced the rise of the "platonic mode" to the ideals of the *précieuses* that arrived in England with Queen Henrietta Maria. Harbage quotes this definition of platonic love from a private letter of 1634: "it is a Love abstracted from all corporeal gross Impressions and sensual Apetite, but consists in Contemplations and Ideas of the Mind, not in any carnal Fruition."[23] An early—and skeptical—dramatic treatment of ths theme is Sir William Davenant's *The Platonic Lovers* (1635), in which the lovers finally abandon platonics for marriage. In Centlivre's play, Lucinda imposes a platonic relationship on Belvil, making him swear that "our Conversation is only Friendship. . . . I admire the Beauties of your mind—without regarding those of your Person—Protest I have no Desire to Kiss those rosie Lips—" and so on.[24] But the "platonic" theme is important only in this one scene between Belvil and Lucinda. Elsewhere in the play, Lucinda behaves very much like earlier heroines of the coquette-prude type.

The weakness of *The Platonic Lady* is that its medley of themes, modes, and incidents is never satisfactorily focused. Each of the three strands of the play's action is located in a distinct dramatic world with its own conventions and expectations. There is first the never-never land of recovered brothers and platonic lovers that Lucinda lives in. Then there is the mercenary world of the London marriage market, manipulated by the marriage broker, Mrs. Brazen. Somewhere between the two is the decidedly theatrical world of Isabella with disguises, mysterious entrances, and sudden exits.

The "platonic" theme has already been discussed. The other parts of the play are in fact more interesting. The Dowdy world is vigorously satiric and broadly comic. It is the most fully realized social milieu in the play and one of Centlivre's best evocations of the disreputable substratum of fashionable life. Mrs. Dowdy is just up from Somerset. She speaks in a farcical regional dialect and there is a good deal of fun at her expense as she awkwardly tries to metamorphose herself into a fashionable and accomplished beauty (pp. 29–34). Also belonging to this world are Sharper and his servant Equipage. The play begins with an amusing scene in which Sharper cheats Equipage out of his back wages (pp. 1–4). Centlivre liked this scene well enough to rework and reuse part of it in *The Perplexed Lovers*. [25]

Some characteristic Centlivre comedy of intrigue is provided by Isabella's disguises and stratagems to revive Belvil's love. But the success is in individual scenes rather than in the plot as a whole, which is confused and rather pointless. Isabella was played by Mrs. Oldfield, and the part only really makes sense as a virtuoso showpiece for her, demonstrating her versatility in roles that range from country girl to coquette. Isabella appears first as a wife fleeing from a jealous husband (p. 14); then as the rustic Dorothy (p. 37); then as a fashionable lady jilted by Belvil (p. 56); and finally in her own person (p. 60). The reasons behind this elaborate charade are improbable, even by the standards of the comedy of intrigue.

A final aspect of the play that deserves mention is the character and role of Sir Thomas Beaumont. He is remarkable as Centlivre's only sympathetically conceived father and authority figure. The typical Centlivre father is a tyrant to be tricked or outwitted; or at best a just but unloveable character like Sir Thomas Valere in *The Gamester*. But Sir Thomas Beaumont is a beneficent and kindly Prospero, who manipulates the other characters and the plot. He knows of Belvil's parentage and relationship to Lucinda; he knows about the important papers that Mrs. Dowdy has. Sir Thomas seems out of place in a Centlivre comedy. Centlivre's distrust of fathers and authority figures derives from her Whiggish hatred of absolutism. Her plays constantly stress the importance of personal—and by implication political—liberty. Sir Thomas's exceptional role in *The Platonic Lady* is dictated by the requirements of the plot, but it is still puzzling.

The Platonic Lady was not a popular success. It was produced at the Queen's Theater in the Haymarket on November 25, 1706. Like *The Basset Table*, it ran for only four nights and was never revived. Centlivre's bitterness at this failure is expressed in the Dedication of the play "To all the Generous Encouragers of Female Ingenuity." In this Dedication, Centlivre pleaded for justice against "the Carping Malice of the Vulgar World; who think it a proof of their Sense, to dislike every thing that is writ by Women." Reviewing her own experiences, she recalls her two—anonymous—successes, *Love's Contrivance* and *The Gamester*. She expresses a doubt whether either play would have done so well if their female authorship had been known. She explains the false initials "R.M." signed to the Dedication of *Love's Contrivance* as a trick to conceal the fact that a woman was the author. She also repeats an anecdote told her by the publisher of *The Gamester*. A "Spark" who had seen and liked the play in the theater was about to buy a copy. But his enthusiasm cooled when he enquired who the author was: "being told, a Woman, [he] threw down the Book, and put up his Money, saying, he had spent too much after it already, and was sure if the Town had known that, it wou'd never have run ten days."

After the failure of *The Platonic Lady*, Centlivre's career was at a low ebb. She was the author of eight plays, of which one had been a modest, and one a considerable, success. But her three most recent plays had enjoyed little popular favor. Most of her work had appeared anonymously, and she was oppressed by a feeling of prejudice against her as a woman. But in retrospect we can see that the plaintive Dedication of *The Platonic Lady* marks the end of Centlivre's struggle for recognition. Success was around the corner. Her marriage to Joseph Centlivre in 1707 and the triumph of *The Busy Body* in 1709 proved to be the hinges on which her career was to turn.

CHAPTER 4

The Busy Body

T WO years elapsed between Centlivre's marriage in 1707 and the production of her next play. She put the interval to good use in writing what is probably her best play. *The Busy Body* remained popular with theatergoers on both sides of the Atlantic for over one-hundred-fifty years. Yet this success was not won without a struggle. Mottley tells us that "when it was first offered to the Players, [it] was received very cooly, and it was with great Difficulty that the Author could prevail upon them to think of acting it." During rehearsals Robert Wilks, who was to play the leading role of Sir George Airy, "had so mean an Opinion of his Part . . . that one Morning in a Passion he threw it off the Stage into the Pit, and swore that no body would bear to sit to hear such Stuff." The play was reported to be "a silly thing wrote by a Woman, that the Players had no Opinion of it."[1]

In these inauspicious circumstances, *The Busy Body* was produced at Drury Lane on May 12, 1709. Mottley describes the audience on the first night as "agreeably surprized" by the play.[2] Mottley's account can be confirmed from contemporary sources. In October 1709, the *Female Tatler* reported that at a rehearsal, Wilks had "flung his Part into the Pitt for damn'd Stuff, before the Lady's Face that wrote it."[3] In the *Tatler* for May 14, Steele wrote "this play is written by a lady. In old times we used to sit upon a play here after it was acted; but now the entertainment is turned another way."[4] Steele was obviously thinking of the preproduction prejudice that Mottley describes.

Steele returned to *The Busy Body* in a later *Tatler*. This time he did not merely ask for a fair hearing; he handed down a favorable judgment. The *Tatler* was an influential tastemaker. Steele's praise probably contributed to the play's success: "The plot and incidents of the play are laid with that subtlety of spirit which is peculiar to females of wit, and is very seldom well performed by those of the other sex, in whom craft in love is an act of invention, and not, as with women, the effect of nature and instinct."[5] Steele seems to mean that in *The Busy Body* the incidents and intrigues appear natural, not forced. A man writing the same kind of play would have had to invent the stratagems, which would consequently have appeared contrived. Steele's point is not very convincing. It is hard to believe that a man could not have written *The Busy Body*. But it was traditional to praise women writers for their natural talent rather than their acquired art. Dryden had used the same antithesis as Steele in his ode on Anne Killigrew:

> Art she had none, yet wanted none:
> For Nature did that Want supply,
> So rich in Treasures of her Own,
> She might our boasted Stores defy.[6]

Steele's praise may have gratified Centlivre as a woman: it can hardly have pleased her as a writer.

I   *Plot and Marplot*

As with most of Centlivre's comedies, the plot of *The Busy Body* centers on the problems and intrigues of two pairs of lovers. But contrary to her usual practice, in this play Centlivre pairs sparkish hero with lively heroine and quiet heroine with serious hero. Sir George Airy wants to marry Miranda: her guardian (Sir Francis Gripe) wants to marry her himself. Charles Gripe wants to marry Isabinda: her father (Sir Jealous Traffick) wants her to marry a Spanish merchant. The business of the play is to outwit father and guardian.

The lovers are contrasted in circumstances as well as in character. Sir George is rich and rakish, but he is in some doubt as to whether his love for Miranda is returned. Charles is poor, but he is assured of Isabinda's love. Miranda is dependent on her guardian for her fortune, but she enjoys personal freedom of movement. Isabinda is virtually imprisoned in her father's house. Miranda inevitably appears more active and independent, Isabinda more timid and subdued. Sir George is engaged in a pursuit of Miranda; Charles in the rescue of Isabinda. This makes for greater variety of comic effects than in Centlivre's earlier plays.

The clever and resourceful Miranda is the most memorable of the lovers. It is she who makes the running, and Sir George has to follow where she leads. She is a consummate dissembler, as adept at playing the coquette as at acting the prude. [7] Yet she is neither of these. She is in love with Sir George from the beginning, although she is too prudent to admit as much to him at the outset. Perhaps Steele had her role particularly in mind when he spoke of "craft in love" as "the effect of nature and instinct."

In the subplot, the dominant role is played by Charles. This is necessarily so since Isabinda is immured in her father's house. Sir Jealous Traffick is a retired merchant who lived for many years in Spain. There he contracted an admiration for Spanish customs, especially their treatment of women. There is a similar character in Wycherley's *The Gentleman Dancing Master* (1672), in which James Formal renames himself Don Diego and prides himself on being "as grave, grum, and jealous, as any Spaniard breathing." [8] This is Sir Jealous's character in a nutshell. Centlivre presumably knew Wycherley's play, but she took from it no more than the idea of the Spanish humor. The Spanish treatment of women, especially of daughters before marriage, gives great scope for the writer of the comedy of intrigue. It makes even a lover's access to his mistress a problem of disguise and deception, surreptitious entry, and probably precipitate retreat. In later plays, Centlivre exploited these possibilities more fully: *Marplot* and *The Wonder* are both set in Lisbon, where intrigue and jealousy seem more natural than in London.

Miranda and Sir Jealous are, after Marplot, the most notable characters in the play. The guardian, Sir Francis Gripe, is an avaricious and amorous old man. But he is more of a type, and less well individualized than Sir Jealous. Neither Sir George nor Charles has a very good part. Perhaps this was why Wilks "flung his Part into the Pitt"; only in the "dumb" scene does Sir George have a dominant role.

The Busy Body as described thus far is much like earlier Centlivre comedies. There is the usual quartet of lovers, although there are—untypically—two father figures. But it is the character of Marplot that is the really new and distinctive feature of *The Busy Body*. Marplot is the title character. His peculiar humor is his insatiable and usually unseasonable curiosity. Before *The Busy Body*, Centlivre had used characters like Marplot to provide broader comic fun than the stratagems of the lovers. They were often only minimally involved in the plot, but shown off in static satiric scenes that functioned chiefly to display them. A notable example is Wou'dbe in *Love at a Venture*. His principal scene (pp. 5–9) contributes nothing to the advancement of the action; it serves only to display Wou'dbe's foolishness. Characters like Wou'dbe were usually treated with amused or dismissive contempt.

This type of humor character is represented in *The Busy Body* by Sir Jealous Traffick and Sir Francis Gripe. But in Marplot, Centlivre created a new kind of sympathetic humor character. Nor is Marplot a static or subsidiary character: he is the mainspring of the greater part of the action of the play. There can be little doubt that the character of Marplot was the chief reason for *The Busy Body's* popular success.

Marplot was well calculated to appeal to an age which was beginning to distrust wit and the laughter that derived from what Hobbes had called a "sudden glory arising from some sudden conception of some eminency in ourselves, by comparison with the infirmity of others, or with our own formerly."[9] The triumph of good nature and sympathy over this laughter of "sudden glory" brought about a new kind of humor character, the "amiable humorist." Stuart Tave offers this distinction between the old humor and the new: "Humor is no longer the satirist's carrion, but the expression of good nature. People like Colley Cibber begin to appear, parading their foibles, happy and complacent. . . . This distinguishes [Sir Roger de Coverley, in the *Spectator*] from the humorous characters of Jonson and Shadwell; unlike them he has no directly didactic, satiric function as a comic character."[10]

Centlivre is a transitional figure in this progress from satiric to sympathetic humor. Her earlier plays are notably more astringent than her later ones. The treatment of the guardians in *A Bold Stroke for a Wife* is affable compared to the treatment of Ogle in *A Beau's Duel* or Wou'dbe in *Love at a Venture*. In *The Wonder*, Felix's jealousy is treated not satirically but sympathetically. But Marplot is Centlivre's best "amiable humorist."

Perhaps the crucial factor in the characterization of Marplot is that we are not invited or intended to feel superior to him. This is clear from comparisons with the notable busybodies in restoration comedy who have been proposed as prototypes of Marplot. The comparisons are interesting irrespective of the question of "source."[11] The two are Sir Martin in Dryden's *Sir Martin Mar-All* (1667) and Intrigo in Sir Francis Fane's *Love in the Dark* (1675). Intrigo is actually closer to Sir Politick Would-be in *Volpone* than he is to Marplot. He is a minor character, much occupied with ferreting out state secrets. His inquisitiveness gets him into several scrapes; but unlike Marplot, he is treated with contempt, not sympathy.

Sir Martin Mar-All is concisely described in the list of characters as a "Fool." He is less a busybody than a blunderer, who talks when he should be quiet and who will not listen to advice. There is nothing beguiling or sympathetic about Sir Martin's invincible stupidity. He is harshly treated by Dryden, losing his prospective wife to his clever servant Warner. John Downes recorded that Dryden wrote Sir Martin "purposely for the Mouth of Mr. Nokes."[12] Cibber's description of Nokes's acting gives us a good idea of how contemporary audiences saw Sir Martin: "he had a shuffling Shamble in his Gait, with so contented an Ignorance in his Aspect, and an aukward Absurdity in his Gesture, that had you not known him, you cou'd not have believ'd, that naturally he could have had a Grain of common Sense."[13] It is clear that we are intended to feel superior to Sir Martin; that the laughter he provokes derives from a "sudden glory."

Marplot's humor is his inquisitiveness: "Lord, Lord, how little Curiosity some People have! Now my chief Pleasure lies in knowing every Body's Business" (p. 28). It appears an amiable humor because it is so frank, active, and disinterested. Centlivre prevents Marplot appearing merely absurd or stupid by endowing him with a lively curiosity, an engaging lack of foresight, and an open good nature. He is also generous and anxious to help his friends. He often gets into scrapes through his misdirected efforts to do them a good turn. He is often tactless, impudent, obsessive, officious, and inept. But it is impossible to remain angry with him for long, as Sir George and Charles find at the end of the play:

Sir George. Thou hast been an unlucky Rogue.
Marplot. But very honest.
Charles. That I'll vouch for; and freely forgive thee. (P. 71)

The "amusing but inoffensive Marplot," as Jess Byrd calls him, is obviously "designed not for reform but for laughter."[14]

II   *St. James's Park*

The Busy Body is worth examining in some detail as perhaps the best example of Centlivre's dramatic technique. One of her most enjoyable plays, it is also a triumph of construction, timing, and the disposition of comic business. Like all Centlivre's full length plays, *The Busy Body* is divided into five acts. But the construction and balance of *The Busy Body* are exceptional. Only *A Bold Stroke for a*

Wife is as skillfully composed. *The Busy Body* consists of an act of exposition, three acts of complication, and a final act of unraveling. The two major comic scenes—the "dumb" scene and the "monkey" scene—are so placed as to balance each other, in the first half of Act II and the second half of Act IV. Proper attention is paid throughout the play to the provision of necessary "bridge" scenes, to the modulation of tension, and to the varying of the pace of the action.

The first act of *The Busy Body* takes place in St. James's Park at an unfashionable hour of the morning: an ideal time and place for both the chance encounter and the discreet appointment. Two friends, both on errands of love, meet accidentally. They compare notes on their situations and plans. Sir George Airy is a man of independent fortune: 4,000 a year. He is engaged in two affairs. He has made an assignation in the park with a masked *incognita* who is clever and witty; but he is more deeply involved with a woman whom he has admired by sight but not spoken with. The latter is Miranda, the ward of Sir Francis Gripe. Sir George's friend is Charles Gripe, Sir Francis's son. Charles is in love with Isabinda, the daughter of a rich merchant—Sir Jealous Traffick. She returns his love, but her father disapproves of Charles as a son-in-law. Instead, he is determined that she shall marry a Spanish merchant.

The characters and circumstances of the two men are rapidly developed (pp. 1–3). Marplot, who is to be the play's driving comic force, is introduced. We do not see him in action this early in the play, but Charles tells an anecdote that gives us some idea of what to expect in the way of comedy from Marplot: "I had lent a certain Merchant my hunting Horses, and was to have met his wife in his Absence: Sending him along with my Groom to make the Complement, and to deliver a Letter to the Lady at the same time; what does he do, but gives the Husband the Letter, and offers her the Horses" (p. 6). Charles's servant Whisper brings word that Isabinda has been prevented from meeting him in the park. The three men go their separate ways. The tone and social milieu of the play have been set, and we know what kind of comedy to expect.

The second scene combines development with further exposition. Miranda arrives in the park and meets Isabinda's maid, Patch. This second accidental rencontre parallels the first. Isabinda's plight is sketched in more detail and is graphically illustrated by her inability to come to the park as arranged. The comparative situations of the two women are discussed, as those of the men had been earlier. The action proper of the play begins with Sir George's reentry with Sir

Francis Gripe (p. 9). Miranda and Patch withdraw out of sight but not out of earshot. Sir George is trying to arrange for Sir Francis to let him speak with Miranda. A hundred guineas is agreed on for an interview. [15] This clear breach of his trust as a guardian establishes Sir Francis as both venal and stupid. He can see in the proposal neither immorality nor danger to his own plans. He is foolishly deluded by Miranda's pretended fondness for him.

A notable feature of this scene is Miranda's succession of peeping asides. In about two pages of text (pp. 9–10), Miranda eight times peeps out of hiding and makes a remark aside. This convention may seem strange to modern readers, but Centlivre's contemporaries accepted it as a common dramatic technique. In this scene, the peeping asides function as comic punctuation. Some of Miranda's remarks are replies to Sir George or Sir Francis, others are serious statements of her real feelings about the two men. One aside is both comic and serious:

Sir Francis . . . in sober Sadness she cannot abide 'em [young men].
Miranda. (Peeping.) In sober Sadness you are mistaken—. (P. 9)

Here Miranda is obviously intended to mimic Sir Francis's intonation; but she is also telling the truth. This combination of jest and earnest is characteristic of her. Outraged by the bargain the two men are driving about her—as though she were some piece of property to be bartered—she promises to "fit you both" (p. 10). Thus, unexpected developments are foreshadowed in the approaching interview that Sir George has bought.

Sir Francis leaves with Sir George's guineas. Miranda and Patch come forward. Miranda is masked, and Sir George is therefore unaware that he is now enjoying gratis what he has just paid a hundred guineas to enjoy later. In this scene, Miranda plays the coquette (pp. 10–13). There is an amusing duel of wit as Sir George tries to persuade her to unmask. Finally she agrees to, if he will turn his back. He does so and Miranda and Patch promptly slip out. For about half a minute, Sir George keeps up a running commentary as though Miranda were still present; finally the suspicious silence prompts him to turn round. First Miranda was heard but not seen; then spoken to but not present. Both the concealment and the disappearing trick develop Miranda's character as resourceful and elusive. The act ends with Sir George abashed but determined to intensify his pursuit.

III   *The "Dumb" Scene*

Act II begins with a short scene (pp. 14–15) between Sir Francis and Miranda. He tells her about his bargain with Sir George. Miranda affects to be amused and to think Sir George an "odious young Fop" (p. 14). In order to prevent Sir George discovering that she is his *incognita* of the park, she proposes to Sir Francis that she should remain dumb throughout the interview. Sir Francis agrees to the stratagem. Our curiosity about the interview is thus heightened. But instead of gratifying us at once, Centlivre suspends the issue for a few pages (pp. 15–19). Sir Francis is now shown to be an unnatural father as well as a venal guardian. Charles enters in a vain attempt to appeal to his father for financial support. The best that Sir Francis will do is suggest that Charles should find a wealthy wife—such as Lady Wrinkle (p. 18). He offers to introduce Charles to her for nothing, even though a matchmaker would charge twenty guineas for the service. Sir Francis's calm acceptance of this traffic in marriage is of a piece with his sale of an interview with Miranda.

Sir Francis is also Marplot's guardian. It is therefore no surprise when Marplot enters, having followed Charles from the park. Marplot is a static character, but Centlivre develops his role slowly. In Act I he was merely inquisitive; in this scene we find him actively running about after Charles. Only in Act III and later is comic capital made out of his humor. Consequently, we do not tire of him as we might have done if his blunders had been introduced too soon and repeated too often. The economy of Centlivre's construction is seen in the threefold purpose that his brief scene serves: it increases the tension, shows another side to Sir Francis's character, and develops the role of Marplot.

As soon as Charles and Marplot are disposed of, Sir George arrives for his interview (pp. 19–24). Sir Francis remains in the room but out of hearing. Sir George begins by declaring his love in some prepared speeches. Miranda's silence provides a test of his resourcefulness. First he gets Miranda to reply to his questions with a system of nods, shakes of the head, and sighs (p. 21). Then in a virtuoso improvisation, he asks his questions and answers them himself on Miranda's behalf (pp. 22–23). He even composes an extempore letter and a song to himself. The "dumb" scene is punctuated in two ways: by Miranda's asides and by Sir Francis's interruptions. Miranda's asides work in much the same way as in the scene in the park. Sir Francis is presumably stationed in a remote area of the stage; on three occasions he runs up to the couple, disturbed at the turn affairs appear to be taking, and has to be repelled by Sir George. The asides and the interruptions prevent the scene from becoming monotonous without dissipating the rising tension. When Sir George's time has expired, Miranda silently withdraws. Sir George and Sir Francis have a brief talk. Miranda's ascendency over both men has been confirmed: neither knows what she is really about. Sir George is baffled, but cannot really believe that she intends to marry Sir Francis. Sir Francis is complacent, seeing nothing strange in Miranda's declared preference for himself. Both men exit with sets of couplets (p. 24). The midact couplets serve to emphasize a pause and a break in the action as we move to Sir Jealous Traffick's house and the Spanish plot.

The "dumb" scene is a variant on a comic situation that had been used by both Boccaccio and Ben Jonson: in the fifth tale of the third day of *The Decameron,* and in Act I, Scene vi of *The Devil Is an Ass.* Ben Jonson's editors, Herford and Simpson, think that Centlivre used Boccaccio because "In Boccaccio the interview is not in the hearing of the husband; Jonson has changed this in order to make Fitzdottrel look a more consummate fool."[16] Actually, Centlivre's scene is a further refinement on Jonson's, not a return to Boccaccio's. Sir Francis's interruptions—which naturally have no counterpart in Boccaccio, where the husband is not in the room—parallel Fitzdottrell's intrusions into Wittipol's conversation with his wife. In *The Devil Is an Ass,* Fitzdottrell stands close by; Centlivre improved the theatrical possibilities of the scene by making Sir Francis run backwards and forwards.

In both Boccaccio and Jonson, the silence is enjoined by the husband. The moral point is that the husband thinks that the letter of imposing silence is more important than the spirit of pimping—for that is what it amounts to—for their wives. Jonson indeed makes Fitzdottrell "the more consummate fool," notably by allowing him to expose his own folly in a long speech of intended self-justification. Jonson makes the scene a searching critique of marital responsibility. Centlivre changed both the emphasis and the morality by giving the idea of not speaking to Miranda herself; in addition, Miranda is not the wife but the ward of Sir Francis. These changes complicate the intrigue while they simplify the morality. Sir George is engaged on a legitimate courtship, not on a cuckolding expedition. The moral condemnation falls entirely on Sir Francis. At the same time, neither Sir George nor Sir Francis really knows what Miranda is up to. In Boccaccio and Jonson, the wife was a pawn between the two men. In

The Busy Body, it is Miranda who is in control: she "fits" the two men as she had earlier promised herself that she would.

IV   *The Plot Thickens*

Contemporary audiences would have seen *The Busy Body* with brief intervals between each act. These intervals would have been enlivened by some musical or other entertainment. But for convenience of discussion, the middle part of the play—between the "dumb" scene and the "monkey" scene—can be considered as a whole. This central section comprises four main sequences and two bridge scenes. Sandwiched between the two major scenes involving Miranda and Sir George, this part of the play is primarily concerned with the Charles-Isabinda plot. Act II is completed by the first scene at Sir Jealous's house and a short bridge scene at Charles's lodgings. Act III consists of a second scene at Sir Jealous's, a scene at Sir Francis Gripe's, and a bridge scene in a tavern. Act IV begins with a third scene at Sir Jealous's, and is completed by the "monkey" scene. Centlivre's care in the construction of the play is evident from this summary.

The first scene at Sir Jealous's house is slow-moving, providing a change of pace from the bustling "dumb" scene. Its purpose is largely expository: it introduces us to Sir Jealous and his Spanish humor. Whisper and Patch arrange for Charles to visit Isabinda as soon as Sir Jealous has gone out. Unluckily Sir Jealous sees Whisper, and his suspicions are aroused. This prepares us for his later unexpected return. As so often in Centlivre, developments that surprise the characters in the play are foreseen by the audience. Centlivre generally prefers anticipation to surprise as a dramatic technique.

The scene in Charles's lodgings at the end of the act (pp. 27–29) has two functions. Whisper brings Charles news of the appointment with Isabinda. More importantly, it contributes to the characterization of Marplot. The scene shows him at his best and worst. It begins with Marplot advancing Charles a loan; this is one instance when he is genuinely serviceable to his friends. But the scene ends with Marplot's exasperating refusal to take no for an answer when Charles will not let him into the secret of his assignation with Isabinda. Marplot secretly determines to follow him; this will lead to the first comic disaster in the next act. Sir George also has a small part in this scene. His presence helps prevent the two parts of the play from moving too far apart.

Act III has two comic sequences, both involving Marplot and his blunders. Faster moving than Act II, it represents an increase in the play's momentum. The first sequence concerns Charles and Isabinda. Charles arrives at the street outside Sir Jealous's house. Patch lets him in. Marplot arrives just too late, but decides to wait about on the off chance of something interesting happening. The scene changes to the inside of the house for a brief scene between Charles and Isabinda—the first in the play (pp. 30–31). But their protestations of love are interrupted by Patch's news that Sir Jealous is coming back (p. 31). Patch conducts Charles out through the balcony. The scene changes back to the street.[17] Sir Jealous arrives, and Marplot overhears him threaten to "make Mince-Meat" of any man he finds in the house (p. 32). Marplot thinks he will do Charles a service by telling Sir Jealous that "the Gentleman you threaten is a very honest Gentleman" and not without friends. Of course this merely confirms Sir Jealous's suspicions. He beats Marplot for his pains and goes into the house. Charles drops down from the balcony and finds Marplot. Charles thinks that it was Marplot who alarmed Sir Jealous and exits in high dudgeon. But in fact Marplot did Charles a service by detaining Sir Jealous in the street. Here Marplot appears as, for once, more sinned against than sinning. His efforts get him nothing but hard blows from Sir Jealous and hard words from Charles. The whole episode is rounded off by a brief scene inside the house (pp. 33–34) in which Sir Jealous upbraids Isabinda and threatens her with an imminent Spanish husband. As in the middle of Act II (p. 24), a decisive break in the action is signaled by Isabinda's final speech in couplets (p. 34).

The scene changes to Sir Francis's house. Sir Francis and Miranda are discussing the "dumb" scene and their approaching—as Sir Francis thinks—marriage (pp. 34–36). Miranda uses Sir Francis's good temper to get him to promise her his written consent to marry whom she pleases. She tells him that this is merely to prove that she marries him freely. They are interrupted by Marplot (p. 36). As in the previous scene, Marplot combines good intention with inept execution. Here he acts as Sir George's advocate to Miranda; he has of course no inkling of her real feelings for Sir George. The resourceful Miranda puts Marplot to use, just as she has made Sir Francis her unwitting agent in the first part of the scene. She gives Marplot a message for Sir George: that his suit is hopeless and that he should "keep from the Garden Gate on the left Hand; for if he dares to saunter there, about the Hour of Eight, as he used to do, he shall be saluted with a Pistol or a Blunderbuss" (p. 38). Miranda hopes that Sir George will take the hint and come. Neither Marplot nor Sir Francis suspects her real purpose. Here again, as in the "dumb" scene, Miranda manipulates and makes fools of two men at the same time.

Act III, like Act II, ends with a bridge scene (pp. 39–42). This time the location is a tavern. Once again Sir George and Charles are engaged in a discussion of their affairs. Marplot is prudent enough to send a message to test his welcome from Charles before joining them (p. 40). He apologizes to Charles and gives Sir George the message from Miranda. Charles writes a letter to Isabinda and gives it to Whisper to deliver to Patch. Uncharacteristically, Charles offers Marplot his company home: the unwonted attention makes Marplot suspect that there is more to the affair of the garden gate than he had supposed. Charles, of course, hopes to be able to keep Marplot from spoiling Sir George's clandestine appointment. But Marplot determines to give Charles the slip and to follow Sir George. The mystery of the garden gate seems more attractive than the mystery of Charles's letter. Thus the act ends with a promise of rapid developments in both actions—Charles's new appointment with Isabinda, and Sir George's assignation at the garden gate. We can look forward to Marplot's unseasonable presence at one of these at least.

The first half of Act IV (pp. 43–51) is a more dramatic rerun of the earlier scene at Sir Jealous's (pp. 29–34). Again, there are rapid changes of scene between the street and the inside of the house. We begin in the street. Whisper brings Charles's letter and gives it to Patch. Patch unluckily drops it for Sir Jealous to pick up on his return (p. 43). Sir Jealous is alarmed, cancels his engagements, and orders his supper to be laid in Isabinda's room—the better to keep watch over her. There is no opportunity for the appointment with Charles to be canceled: no sooner is Patch's loss discovered that Sir Jealous arrives with it. Since the letter in in cipher, Patch makes a shift to pretend that it is her "Charm for the Tooth-ach" (p. 46). The immediate crisis is averted; but Sir Jealous's suspicions have not been totally allayed. The tension increases as we begin to watch for Charles's arrival. Sir Jealous has Patch sing and Isabinda accompany her on the spinet. They are nervous and therefore "horribly out of Tune." Just as Sir Jealous is losing his temper, Charles steps out of the closet, suspecting nothing (p. 48). He retreats at once when he sees Sir Jealous; Isabinda pretends to faint in front of the closet door. By the time Sir Jealous can get into the closet Charles is safely off. Sir

Jealous summarily expels Patch from the house. Outside she meets Charles. As usual, out of the ashes of one plot another plot is born. Patch gives Charles the idea of impersonating the Spanish merchant that Sir Jealous is expecting. She and Charles go out on a happier note (p. 51).

V *The "Monkey" Scene*

The second part of Act IV (pp. 51–58) begins outside the garden gate. Sir George has kept his appointment, and Miranda's maid Scentwell lets him in and conducts him to her mistress. We move into the house. Miranda has a brief soliloquy (p. 51) in which she justifies her actions to herself. Sir George arrives, and he and Miranda have their first serious conversation (pp. 52–53). Their talk confirms that Miranda is neither a coquette nor a prude but a woman of sense. They are interrupted by Scentwell's news that Sir Francis (and Marplot) are coming into the house. Thus far—in the surreptitious entry, the serious conversation between the lovers, and the interruption—the scene parrallels the sequence in Act III with Charles and Isabinda (pp. 29–33). But here Centlivre develops the comedy along a different line.

Sir George does not leave as Charles had done: instead, he is hidden behind the chimneyboard. Sir Francis enters with Marplot. Sir Francis had been on his way to Epsom. He has returned at Marplot's behest to warn Miranda not to shoot Sir George if he should fail to disregard the warning (p. 54). Thus once again, it is Marplot who is responsible for the unseasonable interruption. The main comedy of the scene, however, develops from the fact that Sir Francis enters "peeling an Orange." The peel has to be disposed of and the fireplace—where Sir George is hiding—is the obvious spot. Scentwell tries to avert the discovery of Sir George by asking for the peel to eat. Sir Francis refuses, saying that she has the "Green Pip" already. The tension mounts as Sir Francis approaches the chimney. Miranda in turn tries to avert the crisis: she tells Sir Francis that she has a pet monkey shut up in the chimney. This is not so far from the truth. Sir Francis believes her and gives the peel to Scentwell to dispose of. But the crisis is prolonged: inquisitive Marplot wants to see the monkey, and it is all Sir Francis and Miranda can do to keep him away from the chimney. Eventually Sir Francis's coach is announced, and all seems to be well. But Marplot contrives to stay behind a moment and lifts up the chimneyboard. Discovering Sir George without seeing who he is, Marplot cries out "Thieves, Thieves, Murder!" and Sir Francis rushes back.

Luckily Marplot manages to save the awkward situation that he has precipitated. Before Sir Francis is back, Sir George runs out. On his way he breaks some china ornaments; Marplot invents a story that the "monkey" was responsible and has escaped through the window. Obviously, rapid pace and sharp timing are essential to the effectiveness of this scene, which is one of the best in the play. Each peak of tension must be greater than the last, and the speed of action must accelerate. Sir Francis finally leaves, and Sir George returns. The tension relaxes. Patch comes in with news of what has happened at Sir Jealous's. Marplot is anxious to meddle with Charles's affairs, but Miranda and Sir George keep him with them. This part of the scene (pp. 56–58), after the final exit of Sir Francis, has the same function as the bridge scenes that concluded Acts II and III. Future developments are foreshadowed but not revealed in detail. At the end of Act III Marplot was anxious to shadow Sir George; at the end of Act IV he is just as keen to be after Charles. At this point, the outwitting of Sir Francis is virtually completed; the final act will concentrate once again on Sir Jealous.

VI   *The Unraveling*

By the end of Act IV, the resources of the comedy of concealment and inopportune entry have been exploited to the full. For the last act, Centlivre changes to a comedy of disguise. Between Acts IV and V, Sir George and Miranda are married. Act V begins with a sententious exchange between Miranda and Patch on the "strange bold thing" that Miranda has just done (p. 58). Patch voices Centlivre's modest but sensible approach to marriage: "it is impossible a Man of Sense shou'd use a Woman ill, indued with Beauty, Wit and Fortune. It must be the Lady's fault, if she does not wear the unfashionable Name of Wife easie, when nothing but Complaisance and good Humour is requisite on either side to make them happy" (p. 58). Miranda is congratulating herself on her escape from her guardian when Sir Francis himself enters. The momentary awkwardness passes; the resourceful Miranda soon adapts her plan to suit the unexpected event. She and Patch had been going to Sir Jealous's; Miranda simply determines to take Sir Francis with them. Miranda tells Sir Francis "positively this is my Wedding Day" (p. 60). The deluded knight supposes that Miranda intends to marry him after they have witnessed the wedding at Sir Jealous's.

The scene changes for the last time, to Sir Jealous's house. Charles and Sir George have disguised themselves as Don Babinetto and his friend Meanwell. Sir Jealous is deceived by the impersonation and drags in Isabinda to be married to the Spanish merchant without delay. Isabinda protests violently and implores pleadingly until Sir George whispers that Don Babinetto is Charles in disguise. Parson Tackum is announced; the party goes offstage for the wedding ceremony. But Marplot has a final plot to mar. He arrives outside Sir Jealous's (p. 56) and alarms a servant with his inquiries after Charles. Marplot is taken in to Sir Jealous, who recognizes him from the incident in Act III. Sir Jealous guesses at the imposture, but not quite in time. Sir George keeps him out with the point of his sword while the parson finishes the ceremony. Sir Francis and Miranda arrive (p. 69). All the plots and secrets come out, including Miranda's marriage to Sir George. A general reconciliation takes place. Only Sir Francis refuses to forgive and join in; he leaves with a "Confound you all!" (p. 71). Like Malvolio at the end of *Twelfth Night*, Sir Francis takes with him all the accumulated strife and bitterness of the play. His departure prepares the way for general concord. Sir Jealous accepts Charles with a good grace; Miranda gives him the papers—kept by Sir Francis—that make him master of his estate. Marplot is forgiven. Whisper and Scentwell are given the choice "to Marry, or keep their Services." Both choose the second option. Sir Jealous invites all to "a chearful Glass, in which we'll bury all Animosities' (p. 72).

The Busy Body is a successful amalgam of the comedy of humors with the comedy of intrigue. There are several memorable characters, and they are well integrated into the busy and bustling plot. The action of the play is certainly not probable, but it is well motivated according to the conventions of its genre. Its comic business is plausibly introduced and skillfully spaced out.[18]

CHAPTER 5

Farces and Spanish Plots

T HERE is no clear line of development to be seen in the plays that Centlivre wrote between *The Busy Body* in 1709 and *The Wonder* in 1714. Bowyer calls the years 1711 and 1712 "a kind of spiritless interlude" for Centlivre.[1] The biographical inference is hardly justified, but the whole period between *The Busy Body* and *The Wonder* could be described as a "spiritless interlude" in her literary career. One of the four plays that were produced during these years is a sprightly farce, but the three full length comedies are all disappointing.

The Man's Bewitched (1709) is a farcical comedy of English provincial life: but it is neither an effective farce nor a good comedy. Much more successful is *A Bickerstaff's Burying* (1710), a one act farce with no pretensions to being a comedy. In *Marplot* (1710), Centlivre took some of the characters from *The Busy Body* to Lisbon and involved them in a new series of adventures. Like most sequels, it is inferior to its original. *Marplot* has an intrigue plot of the "Spanish" kind. In *The Perplexed Lovers* (1712), Centlivre tried to domesticate a Spanish intrigue to an English setting. In the Preface she confessed that "most of the Plot was taken from a Spanish Play." The particular source has not been identified.

I The Man's Bewitched *(1709)*

The Man's Bewitched: or, The Devil to Do about Her was produced at the Queen's Theater in the Haymarket on December 12, 1709. It had a disappointing run of only three nights. When the play was published, Centlivre wrote in the Preface that it had "met with a kind Reception in general" and that it had been well acted. She ascribed the play's short run to the "Pique" of the actors at a paragraph that appeared in the *Female Tatler* for December 12–14.[2]

The *Female Tatler* was one of several rivals—or rather

imitations—of the original *Tatler*. At the time of *The Man's Be-witched*, it was supposedly edited by a "Society of Ladies." Who really wrote the paper is still something of an open question. The issue published on December 14 (No. 69) includes a feature about Centlivre. In keeping with the fiction of the "Society of Ladies," Centlivre is represented as visiting the society and staying to supper with them. After complimenting Centlivre on her new play, the society "had the Curiosity of knowing the Nature of introducing a Play into the House." Centlivre obliges them with a mildly satirical account of the difficulties faced by an author in getting a play produced. According to Centlivre in her Preface, the actors were offended and stopped the run of her play out of spite. Centlivre denied any responsibility for the story in the *Female Tatler*, making the point that "nothing but an Idiot wou'd express themselves so openly" and put "those People out of Humour, whose Action was to give Life to the Piece."

It has been suggested that Centlivre was for a time joint editor and author of the *Female Tatler* with Bernard Mandeville.[3] In fact, it seems quite unlikely that Centlivre had anything to do with the paper, much less that she was ever an editor. Although the paragraph in the issue of December 14 seems at first sight to be a puff for *The Man's Bewitched*, and has been read as such by Bowyer and others, the "praise" must really be intended ironically. Centlivre herself was obviously not flattered by it when, in her Preface, she asked the *Female Tatler* "to be Witty no more at my Expence." For the *Female Tatler* singled out for praise some of the weakest scenes in the play. No one could really have thought that *The Man's Bewitched* had "a better Plot" than *The Busy Body*. The following "praise" must also be ironic: "nor is Mrs. Saunders [who played the servant Dorothy], tho' ranked below Belinda [the leading woman], to be less applauded for her Natural Trembling and Faultering in her Speech when she apprehended Sir Jeffery to be a Ghost." This is a sample of the scene in question: "I, I, I, I, I, o, o, o, o, Roger—Ha, ha, have a care, ca, care—Don't yo, yo, you come near him—Nor let him to, to, to, touch you, even with his Little Finger—. . . . Ay, bo, bo, bo, but we, we, know you, you, you, a, a, a, a, are not so, Sir—."[4] Pretending that this feeble fooling is one of the best things in the play is indeed being witty at the author's expense.

The conspicuous inferiority of *The Man's Bewitched* to *The Busy Body* is easy to see. In the earlier play there were two complementary and well-balanced actions linked through the character of Marplot. In

The Man's Bewitched, the three plots are linked only by some of the characters knowing each other. In the first plot, Captain Constant has spread a report that his father is dead and comes to Peterborough to trick his father's steward out of half a year's rent and his daughter.[5] The imposition succeeds until his father's unexpected arrival in Act V. By then Constant has married Belinda. When his father—Sir Jeffry Constant—does arrive, he is taken at first for a ghost. The confusion is ironed out, and at the end of the play, he is reconciled to his son's marriage by the news that Belinda is not Trusty's daughter at all, but a noble foundling with an independent fortune. This part of the play is largely borrowed from Hauteroche's *Le Deuil* (1672). Centlivre added the fact of Belinda's noble birth and the rustics Num and Slouch. Num is the son of a local landowner and a would-be suitor to Belinda; Slouch is his servant.

The nominal second plot supplies both the title and the subtitle of the play. Faithful and Laura have long been in love, but she is closely confined by her guardian. Sir David Watchum wants to marry her himself. This part of the play is based on Regnard's *Les Folies amoureuses* (1704). Centlivre follows Regnard more closely than she does Hauteroche in the main plot. The action is virtually a siege of Sir David's house. In Act II there is an elaborate plot to get Faithful into the house; in Act IV an even more elaborate one to get Laura out. Sir David's words that there is "the Devil to do about her" (p. 40)—alluding to the difficulty he has getting Faithful out of his house without meeting Laura—prove prophetic. In Act IV she pretends to be mad, and there really is "the Devil to do." Faithful's servant Manage assumes the part of an exorcist and affects to draw the "Devil" out of Laura and into Faithful. Laura's servant Lucy cries out "the Man's bewitch'd" (p. 53). In the confusion that ensues, Laura and Faithful escape. The third plot is a slight pendant to the first two. Lovely wants to marry Maria, who is a coquette-prude. She stubbornly holds out—for no particular reason—for four acts and capitulates for no better reason at the end of the play.

The Man's Bewitched does not make a very good reading play. The actions are developed mechanically, and there is too much farcical business. The main characters are not well individualized. The servants, however, are well drawn and lively. The witty Clinch and the resourceful Manage are indeed more vigorous and amusing than their masters. Manage has a particularly good scene with Sir David (pp. 14–17). Manage was played by Cibber, who specialized in this kind of impudence. Centlivre may have written the scene with

Cibber in mind: it is amusing, but it does not contribute much to the development of the play.

The principal farcical scenes are Laura's madness in Act IV and the "ghost" scene in Act V. It is difficult to judge how effective they would have been on the stage. In reading, both scenes seem too long. Laura's madness (pp. 48–53) inevitably suffers from comparison with Valentine's in *Love for Love*. In the Preface to *The Man's Bewitched,* Centlivre tells how the "ghost" scene had been the subject of some dispute before the play was produced. She says that she willingly shortened it at Cibber's request—"because too much repetition is tiresome"—but that she felt compelled to object when another actor, Estcourt, "slic'd most of it out." The printed text presumably represents either the original state of the scene or the Cibber-inspired shortening. The company as a whole, apparently, agreed to the Cibber compromise, and the "ghost" scene was much applauded in the theater. Modern readers will probably agree with Estcourt. The scene is too long (pp. 58–62), and the comic point could perhaps have been made more effectively in a scene of a few lines.

The most successful parts of the play are the elements of local color that Centlivre added to her borrowed French plots. Bowyer calls them "merely a thin veneer with which she covers her borrowing from the French," but they are actually the only vital parts of the play.[6] Num, Slouch, and Roger will bear comparison with the rustic characters in Farquhar's plays of provincial life, *The Recruiting Officer* (1706) and *The Beaux' Stratagem* (1707). Num and Slouch have a solidity that Constant and Faithful lack. This is probably because they speak in a distinctive broad dialect without being patronized at all by Centlivre. She makes them unsophisticated, but not contemptible.

There is an excellent short scene between Roger and Sir Jeffry (pp. 54–55). The incident occurs just before the "ghost" scene. Roger is one of Sir Jeffry's tenants, but does not know him by sight. When he meets Sir Jeffry, whom he believes to be dead, he does not take him for a ghost. Instead, when the two meet outside Trusty's, Roger simply wonders who the rude and self-important stranger can be. Sir Jeffry expects to be deferred to, so there follows an amusing comedy of errors. The scene brings out how remote a landlord Sir Jeffry has been and how soon he has been forgotten.

The Man's Bewitched did not itself become a regular part of the repertory. But the popular appeal of the farcical scenes is attested by the fact that the play was twice quarried by later compilers of farces.

As *The Witchcraft of Love,* it was included in a collection of drolls, *The Strollers' Packet Opened* (1742).[7] The author did a good job, omitting the Lovely-Maria subplot and several unnecessary scenes. A second adaptation (also anonymous) was more drastic. *The Ghost* (1767) retains only the Constant-Belinda plot. *The Ghost* is a trifling piece, but *The Witchcraft of Love*—like the other drolls in the collection—is an excellent farce. Arguably, it is an improvement on its original. *The Man's Bewitched* contains good material for a farce, but as it stands it is a thin comedy.

II   A Bickerstaff's Burying *(1710)*

"The essence of farce," Leo Hughes has suggested, "is its dependence upon mere laughter, as opposed to comedy and its treatment of moral problems."[8] Farce in this sense plays a large part in both *Love's Contrivance* and *The Man's Bewitched.* But in contemporary usage, the division between farce and comedy was more a matter of length than of any critical distinction. A farce was a play in one, two, or more rarely, three acts: but such plays were invariably also "farcical" in the critical sense.

A Bickerstaff's Burying: or, Work for the Upholders, a one act farce, was produced at Drury Lane on March 27, 1710.[9] Its initial run was three nights. Later in the same year, it was published with a satirical dedication that gave extra point to its subtitle. On May 5, 1715, it was revived under the title *The Custom of the Country;* together with *The Busy Body,* it was performed for Centlivre's benefit. It had a few more performances in 1715–1716, but it did not become a stock piece.

The farce is based on an idea taken from the *Arabian Nights.* Sinbad's fourth voyage (Nights 80–82) includes a visit to a country where it is the custom for the surviving partner of a marriage to be buried alive with the deceased spouse. Despite the custom, Sinbad marries. His wife dies, and he is buried with her; but he contrives to escape to tell the tale. Centlivre borrowed only the idea of the "custom": she does not use Sinbad or the story of his adventure.

A Bickerstaff's Burying is set on the island of Cosgar. The farce begins with a graphic representation of a storm and a near ship-wreck.[10] The first scene begins with an encounter between two inhabitants of the island—Lady Mezro and her niece Isabinda—and some of the sailors. The ship is an English one, and Lady Mezro recognizes the captain. She was formerly Mrs. Take-it of Covent

Garden; she was shipwrecked on Cosgar en route to Madras to find a husband. She is now married to a local emir. The scene develops a contrast between the dissatisfaction with Cosgar evident in Lady Mezro and Isabinda—who know the local "custom"—and the enchantment with the island that the sailors express. The sailors' view of the island as an earthly paradise is shattered through a dramatic reversal. News is brought to Lady Mezro that her husband is dying. Instead of reacting to the news with joy and relief—as the sailors expect—Lady Mezro is distraught at the possibility of being buried alive. Her unexpected reaction gives Centlivre an opportunity to introduce some satirical reflections on the common sincerity of mourning wives in England. Lady Mezro goes off to attend her husband. Isabinda stays behind and plots with the English captain how she and her aunt can escape from the hated island.

The second scene shows Lady Mezro at her husband's sickbed. In fact, he had not really been ill, only shamming in order to revive his wife's flagging affection for him. Her arrival and concern improve him visibly; he hints that he wants to be alone with her. Lady Mezro is trying to dissuade him from any rash exertions when the captain comes in and tells her his plot. This is put into action at once. Lady Mezro faints. The situation of husband and wife is immediately reversed: the emir leaps from his couch and calls for servants and medical advice. But Lady Mezro appears to be beyond help. The servants bring in instead two coffins. The emir rushes out in confusion; Lady Mezro, the captain, and Isabinda are left to make their escape.

In the third scene, we leave the adventure of Lady Mezro and return to the sailors. The ship has been repaired, and the sailors are returning on board. A sailor who, in the first scene, had asked the captain for his discharge in order to marry a rich Cosgarian lady, now tells the lady that Cosgar and its "custom" are not for him. He returns on board, leaving the lady and her jewels on shore. A second sailor, more enterprising, arrives. He takes the war into the enemy's camp and persuades the lady to come with him on board, bringing her jewels and leaving Cosgar in favor of England. The amusing transfer of the role of siren from the lady to the sailor reinforces the farce's patriotic theme—that an Englishman and his liberty are more precious than Cosgarian wealth and servitude.

In the final scene, the emir is about to be encoffined. His last wish is to see his wife once more. Her coffin is opened and found to be empty. The happy discovery that his wife is not, after all, dead is confirmed by the news that the English ship has set sail—with his wife, his niece, and his jewels. The emir regards his escape as cheaply bought and prudently resolves not to remarry: "The Laws of Wedlock all Men think severe,/But 'tis Damnation sure to marry here".[11]

A *Bickerstaff's Burying* is thus a well-constructed farce of situation spiced with satirical reflections and comments. Each scene pivots on a comic reversal, and each is developed from the preceding one. Nor is the farce without a serious side. The theme of the evils of mercenary marriages is introduced by Lady Mezro's plight: She was shipwrecked on her way to India to look for a husband, to meet a worse fate on Cosgar. The theme is continued through the island's "custom," which Centlivre uses as a metaphor for the common English practice of "burying" a young wife with an old husband. The latter situation, or the threat of it, is common in her comedies. Centlivre reinforced the moral in the Dedication.

The Dedication, and the play's original title, take up a satirical theme begun by Steele. Swift had used the name Isaac Bickerstaff as a persona in the pamphlets attacking Partridge the astrologer. The character was taken up and developed by Steele when he published the *Tatler* under the name of Isaac Bickerstaff. One of Steele's recurrent themes in the *Tatler* was the idea of burying people who are alive to no purpose—the "walking dead" as he called them. At the end of the first *Tatler*, Steele warned his readers that he would "from time to time print bills of mortality; and I beg the pardon of all who shall be named therein, if they who are good for nothing shall find themselves in the number of the deceased."[12]

The "upholders" (or undertakers) were brought into the satire in a later *Tatler*. Bickerstaff, finding that his ridicule has not succeeded in banishing folly and reforming the "walking dead," decided that he will have to "proceed to extremities, and shall give my good friends the Company of Upholders full power to bury all such dead as they meet with, who are within my former descriptions of deceased persons."[13] This announcement was followed by a fictitious letter from the upholders, complaining of the unwillingness of the "dead" to be buried. Not that Steele was really a friend of the undertakers. In *The Funeral* (1701), he had satirized their ostentatious displays of mourning, as well as the frequent insincerity of a mourner's grief. Centlivre uses both themes in A *Bickerstaff's Burying* and its Dedication.

What the farce buries is Lady Mezro's marriage to the emir. The marriage is alive only in name: therefore it is a "Bickerstaff's" burying. In England, wives are "buried" with their husbands during life; in Cosgar, the practice is continued after the husband's death. Centlivre expands the satirical point in the Dedication "To the Magnificent Company of Upholders." The satiric strategy of the Dedication is to affect perplexity in choosing the most appropriate dedicatee for the farce. The first candidates were "all those young Wives who had sold themselves for Money, and been inter'd with Misery, from the first day of their Marriage." This is obviously the situation of Lady Mezro in the play. The second possible group of dedicatees was the "Race of Old Men" who marry young wives. The emir comes in this category. Finally, Centlivre decided that the upholders were the best choice: " 'tis but Reason you should receive some Tribute from us living, who so truly mourn us dead." She concluded with a mock-panegyric on the upholders. Thus, the Dedication is both a sprightly piece of satire in itself and also a serious commentary on the farce's light-hearted treatment of the problems of marital immurement. The moral of the farce is that the English "custom" is scarcely more barbarous than the Cosgarian; there is not much to choose between burying a wife with a dead husband or a living one.

III   Marplot *(1710)*

Marplot: or, The Second Part of "The Busy Body" was produced at Drury Lane on December 30, 1710. As the sequel of a major popular success, it was staged with some lavishness. It was advertised as having "new Dresses and several new Scenes; particularly an intire Sett of a pleasant Wood, painted by Mr. Boul, after the Italian Manner."[14] *Marplot* enjoyed a successful initial run of six nights, but unlike *The Busy Body*, it did not become a standard item in the repertory. Like most sequels, it is inferior to its original: compared to *The Busy Body*, *Marplot* is mechanical in conception and execution.

The aspects of *The Busy Body* that *Marplot* develops are the Spanish plot and theme. Sir Jealous Traffick has died, and Charles has come to Lisbon on some business connected with his father-in-law's estate. Lisbon was a more convenient location for Centlivre than any Spanish city would have been. England was at war with Spain, whereas since the Methuen Treaties of 1703, Portugal had been an important ally and trading partner. Lisbon was therefore a likely city for English merchants to visit. Centlivre was to use it again in *The Wonder*.[15]

To speak of *Marplot*—and *The Perplexed Lovers*—as having
"Spanish" plots is a matter of convenience rather than precision. The
term was loosely used to describe comedies of intrigue, whether or
not they were set in Spain or based on Spanish sources. In "The
Grounds of Criticism in Tragedy" (1679), Dryden spoke slightingly of
"plays after the new model of the Spanish plots, where accident is
heaped upon accident, and that which is first might as reasonably be
last."[16] Dryden's remarks could with some justice be applied to
Marplot and *The Perplexed Lovers*: many of the incidents could be
reversed in order. In these two plays, Centlivre was much less
successful than she had been in *The Busy Body* in developing the plot
naturally and avoiding the appearance of incidents being contrived.

In *Marplot*, Charles has left Isabinda in London, but brought
Marplot with him "to see the Country." In Lisbon, Charles has made
friends with Colonel Ravelin, an English officer, and started an
intrigue with Dona Perriera, the wife of a Portuguese merchant.
Charles explains his cooled passion for his wife in terms that a
restoration hero might have used: "I lov'd her heartily till I married
her . . . but methinks I see her not with half that desire I us'd to do,
when I scal'd her Window for a Kiss."[17] Most of the play is taken up
with his affair with Dona Perriera: but in compliance with the times,
the cuckolding of her husband is never consummated.

Isabinda has not in fact stayed in London, but has followed Charles
secretly to Lisbon. She disguises herself in boy's clothes. She proves
herself a loyal wife when she determines to reclaim her erring
husband. In Act V, it is by her stratagem that Charles is rescued from
Don Perriera's house. As a result, he repents of his intrigue, and his
love for Isabinda is rekindled. This part of the play is slightly
reminiscent of the Amanda-Loveless plot in Cibber's *Love's Last
Shift* (1696). But there are no direct borrowings; the resemblances
are no more than we would expect from the similarity of theme.

Colonel Ravelin, like Sir George Airy in *The Busy Body*, has two
intrigues on his hands. But the colonel is less lucky than Sir George:
the two women turn out to be not the same, but sisters. There is no
real development in this part of the play. There is one scene
dominated by Mlle Joneton (pp. 29–34). Her character is the familiar
coquette-prude. There is also a scene with her sister Marton (pp.
50–56), whose character is dominated by her extravagant jealousy of
her sister. The highlight of the latter scene is actually Marplot's
interruption (p. 52). At the end of the play, Marton enters a convent
to spite the world. Joneton agrees to marry Ravelin, apparently more

for the convenience of rounding off the play than from any real conviction.

The third main element in the play is Marplot, who interferes as much as he can with the affairs of both Charles and Ravelin. Inevitably, Marplot strikes us with less freshness than in *The Busy Body*; but his character has also taken a turn for the worse. Centlivre bothers less with developing his amiable side. His curiosity appears more forced and less attractive and his exploits are less plausibly motivated. He enters down a chimney (p. 16) and from a balcony (p. 52). Both are at comically inopportune moments, but the surprises are less well prepared for than in *The Busy Body*. They are the actions of a mechanical clown, not of a vital and engaging character.

But perhaps the play's most serious defect is the incongruity of its parts. The Marplot episodes are pure farce. Ravelin's and Charles's intrigues are in the same vein of comedy as most of *The Busy Body*. But a quite different note is struck by the serious rescue and reformation of Charles in the last act. The result is a marked inconsistency in the characterization of Charles. Our sympathies are directed toward him in his intrigue with Dona Perriera, but not in his relationship with Isabinda.[18] The morality of the last act seems compromised by the easygoing approval of the intrigues of the first four acts.

These are much like *The Busy Body*. The most important comic scenes are in Act II, where Marplot's arrival down the chimney (p. 16) interrupts Charles's assignation with Dona Perriera; and in Act IV, where his entry through the balcony (p. 52) similarly interrupts Ravelin's assignation with Marton. In Act III Centlivre varies the working of Marplot's insatiable curiosity. An ambush is laid by Don Perriera for his wife's unknown gallant. A letter is sent as a decoy; Marplot pretends that it is for him and is beaten by Don Perriera's hired thugs (pp. 34–35). This is the usual Marplot sequence in reverse. In these four acts, the intrigues are conducted much as in *The Bush Body*: letters are sent and assignations made, delayed, kept, and interrupted.

Where *Marplot* differs radically from *The Busy Body* is in its last act. The situation is that Don Perriera has overheard—but not seen—Charles in a room with his wife. Before interrupting the guilty pair, he decides to send for two priests. His intention is to "have Christian Charity upon their Souls, for I shall have no Mercy upon their Bodies" (p. 50b). Act V begins with "Isabinda in a Perriwig and Night-gown, and two Priests; a sword lying upon the Table" (p. 51b).

This sombre tableau sets the tone for the act. With the aid of the sword and a large charitable donation, Isabinda persuades the two priests to join her plot to save Charles. She changes clothes with one of the priests and goes to confess Charles with the other. The stratagem enables her to change places with him. The real priest, who went in with Isabinda, tells Don Perriera that the supposed guilty pair are actually both women. Don Perriera's benevolence triumphs over his suspicions, and he accepts the situation with wonder. Everyone assembles in Isabinda'a apartment for a final scene of reconciliation and rejoicing (pp. 58–62).

The greater seriousness of the last act is reflected in Centlivre's manner of staging it. The earlier part of the play was full of rapid exits and entrances: down chimneys, from balconies, through trapdoors. Act V is slower in pace: it is a careful sequence of scenes, each "discovered" by drawing off a pair of back flats to reveal a new scene and group of characters. After the scene with Isabinda and the priests, the sequence of changes is as follows:

Scene, Don Perriera's House. Don Perriera, solus (p. 53b).

Scene draws and discovers Dona Perriera and Charles (p. 53b).

Scene shuts, then draws and discovers Don Perriera listening (p. 54b).

The Scene draws and discovers Dona Perriera on her Knees to Isabinda (p. 55b).

The Scene draws and discovers Charles solus, in Isabinda's Apartment looking about him (p. 58).

These successive discoveries contribute to the calmer and more reflective atmosphere of the act, appropriate to the remorse that is awakened in Charles and Dona Perriera. The discoveries also have an enhanced visual impact. Don Perriera could simply have walked onstage and put his ear to the keyhole. By discovering him in the attitude, Centlivre makes his eavesdropping emblematic. The posture typifies his jealous and mistrustful behavior as a husband. The discovery of Dona Perriera kneeling to Isabinda also has the effect of an allegorical tableau: repentance kneeling before mercy.

A final aspect of *Marplot* that is worth attention is the contrast developed in the play between English and Portuguese society. This is presented largely in terms of liberty and servitude. Women are free in England, confined in Portugal. Centlivre also ridicules Portugal as a priest-ridden society. This is most obvious at the beginning of Act V (pp. 52–53), where Isabinda corrupts the two priests. But the same theme is handled more lightly earlier in the play. Don Perriera finds Marplot in his house in suspicious circumstances; instead of having him instantly dispatched, he sends for a priest with the kind intention of at least saving Marplot's soul (pp. 20–21). Not that Centlivre is uncritical of English society. Dona Perriera draws a contrast that is not much to either country's credit: "a Wound in the Reputation of an English Woman, they say, only lets in Allimony, but with us it lets out life" (p. 15).

IV   The Perplexed Lovers *(1712)*

The Perplexed Lovers was produced at Drury Lane on January 19, 1712. Perhaps partly as a result of the political furore provoked by the original Epilogue—for which see Chapter 1—the play ran for only three nights. It was never subsequently revived. When the play was published, Centlivre's Preface defended the sentiments of the Epilogue with more vigor than the literary merits of the comedy itself. With an air of studied negligence—which perhaps should not be taken at face value—she wrote that she "took very little Pains" with it, "most of the Plot being from a Spanish play." No particular Spanish play has been identified as Centlivre's source, but *The Perplexed Lovers* has a plot that is decidedly "Spanish" in the sense condemned by Dryden. Women are locked up; jealousy and honor are prominent themes; disguises and mistaken identities abound; much of the action takes place in the dark. Throughout the play, "accident is heaped upon accident."

Like *The Man's Bewitched, The Perplexed Lovers* occasioned a preproduction disagreement among the actor-managers. In her Preface, Centlivre tells us that Cibber thought that "the Business wou'd support the Play." But Wilks only agreed that "there was a great deal of Business, but not laughing Business." Even Cibber's more favorable judgment is but faint praise. *The Perplexed Lovers* is certainly one of Centlivre's weakest plays. She herself recognized its defects. In the Preface she acknowledged the excesses of its Spanish plot and promised to "take Care to avoid such Absurdities for the future; and if I live I will endeavour to make my Friends amends in the next." She amply made good this promise with *The Wonder.*

The "perplexed" lovers in the play comprise the usual quartet. Constantia is the serious woman, in love with the serious Colonel Bastion. The difficulty is that her brother Belvil wants her to marry his friend Sir Philip Gaylove (an offstage character); while her father—Sir Roger Merryman—wants her to marry Lord Richlove. Belvil himself is in love with his cousin Camilla, who is the daughter of his uncle Colonel Merryman. Camilla loves Belvil, but she is too much of a coquette to admit it. Belvil is of an unreasonably jealous humor. The contrast between the two actions thus corresponds roughly with that in *The Busy Body* between the pursuit plot and the rescue plot. Belvil pursues Camilla; her coquetry and his jealousy are the main obstacles to be overcome. Bastion has virtually to rescue Constantia from her family; their opposition, not her inclination, is the chief difficulty. Where the quartet differs from the typical pattern in Centlivre's comedies is that the two men are not friends or allies: Belvil is opposed to the idea of his sister marrying Bastion.

There are three amusing servant characters: Florella, Timothy, and Le Front. Florella is Constantia's mercenary maid. She dislikes Bastion because he is not a generous tipper and aids the suit of Lord Richlove, who does know how to fee her properly. There is a strong contrast between the two valets. Timothy is Bastion's servant; he is a coward, but witty and sardonic, like Hector in *The Gamester*. Le Front is Lord Richlove's servant; he too is a coward, but in addition, he is French, vain, and affected. The contrast between them is as much national as personal: Timothy is independent, Le Front servile.

A serious weakness in *The Perplexed Lovers* is that the comic incidents are not sufficiently related to the purpose of the play's action. The problem of bringing the lovers together in marraige is solved rather arbitrarily at the end of the play, instead of being gradually worked out during its whole course. Belvil's opposition to Bastion marrying Constantia, for example, is finally overcome by the device of a letter from Sir Philip Gaylove with the news that he is married. At its best, the comedy of intrigue does without the use of such an awkward *deus ex machina*.

Three of the four principal sources of comedy in *The Perplexed Lovers* are familiar from Centlivre's earlier plays: clash and contrast of character; unexpected arrivals at awkward moments; and the use of disguise. The comic device that Centlivre does not use extensively elsewhere is mistaken identity. Its use in *The Perplexed Lovers* is facilitated by the play's time scheme, specified under the list of characters as "from Five in the Evening 'till Eight in the Morning." Thus, most of the action takes place after dark.

Some scenes are used primarily to develop contrasts between characters. A notable example is the pair of short scenes which open Acts I (pp. 1–4) and II (pp. 12–14).[19] In Act I, the boldness and integrity of Bastion is set against the whining pusillanimity of Timothy. Bastion dominates and is his servant's moral as well as social superior. In Act II, Lord Richlove actually condescends to ask and follow the advice of his French valet Le Front. Here the lord's superiority is a social accident only; he has the soul of a footman. The contrast between the two scenes decisively establishes Bastion as in every way—except wealth—the better man. There is an amusing scene in Act III (pp.25–28) in which Timothy and Le Front meet in the dark. Each is a coward, but hopes that the other is an even greater one. Both put on a brave front; both are in turn surprised at the other's assurance; both back down. This scene is largely to be enjoyed for itself; it does not contribute to the advancing of the action.

The second major source of comedy is the unexpected and inopportune arrival. Bastion can only gain access to Constantia through Camilla's apartment. But since Belvil disapproves of Bastion's suit, he must not know why Bastion visits Camilla so frequently. On two occasions Belvil interrupts Bastion on his way to see Constantia: in Acts I (pp. 5–7) and II (pp. 18–21). Both occasions provide food for Belvil's jealousy. Centlivre avoids the appearance of repetition by varying the situation slightly. In Act I Bastion is actually confronted by Belvil, but manages to invent a plausible excuse about taking leave before going on a journey. In Act II Bastion and Constantia meet in Camilla's room and slip out—seen but not recognized—on Belvil's arrival.

As in *The Busy Body*, the use of disguise occurs chiefly in the last act. As in the earlier play, it makes a welcome change of tempo. Timothy is disguised as a peddler and carries Bastion in his pack. By this means, Bastion is conveyed into Constantia's room (p. 44) despite Belvil's vigilance. Later in the act, Lord Richlove disguises himself as an itinerant coffee vendor (p. 50). In this guise, he too gains admission to Constantia's room. His aim is to ravish her; but Belvil and Bastion have advance warning of the plot and prevent it.

The last major comic device—the one most characteristic of the play—is mistaken identity. In Act I Constantia rushes into the garden and—as she thinks—into Bastion's arms. Actually the waiting figure is not Bastion but Lord Richlove (pp. 9–10). The mistake leads to a temporary estrangement between Constantia and Bastion, who witnessed it. Again in Act III, Constantia mistakes Le Front for Bastion (p.30). Act IV begins with a double instance of the device. Belvil and Constantia meet in the dark. He takes her for Camilla, and she takes him for Bastion. A conversation at total cross-purpose ensues (pp. 31–32). These mistakes are less plausibly contrived than the inopportune arrivals. Centlivre herself recognized this. In *The Wonder*, she developed the comedy of surprise entrance, but suppressed the device of mistaken identity. Its excessive use in *The Perplexed Lovers* was surely one of the "Absurdities" that she apologized for in the Preface.

A serious weakness of *The Perplexed Lovers* is that the same comic incidents are repeated too often. Nor are they well integrated into the total comic structure. In Centlivre's best comedies of intrigue—*The Busy Body* and *The Wonder*—the incidents are coherently ordered and grow out of each other. In *Marplot* and *The Perplexed Lovers*, they often appear forced and arbitrary. Like *Marplot*, *The Perplexed Lovers* contains some amusing scenes and some effective comic business. Yet neither play can be counted a success in dramatic technique. Both plays are marred by structural faults. But these experiments with Spanish plots were useful to Centlivre as a dramatist. With the experience of writing *Marplot* and *The Perplexed Lovers* behind her, she was able in *The Wonder* to produce a satisfying and successful comedy that exploited the strengths and avoided the weaknesses of the earlier Spanish plots.

CHAPTER 6

The Wonder *and Other Plays*

N OTHING that Centlivre wrote between *The Perplexed Lovers* in 1712 and *The Cruel Gift* in 1716 is untouched by politics. Her political opinions and convictions found direct expression in her poems—for which see Chapter 8—and in the Dedication to *The Wonder*, discussed in Chapter 1. But in the four plays that are the subject of this chapter, political themes are indirectly expressed. *The Gotham Election* (1715) is the most overtly political: it is a farce about Tory bribery and Jacobite conspiracy in a small town during a general election. *A Wife Well Managed* (1715) is another farce, this time intended to ridicule the hypocrisy of the Catholic priesthood. *The Wonder* (1714) is a comedy of intrigue, and *The Cruel Gift* (1716) a tragedy of love and honor. At first sight the two plays seem to have little in common; but the central theme in both is freedom, whether personal or political.

These four plays span the whole range of dramatic genres, from tragedy to farce. But behind them all we sense Centlivre's firm Whig convictions. Her hatred of absolutism is seen in her opposition to the tyranny of the father, of the priest, and of the king. On the positive side, Centlivre is a vigorous advocate of personal freedom of choice and action, of religious toleration and liberty of conscience, and of government based on a strictly limited monarchy. These plays are Centlivre's most forceful dramatic expositions of her ideas.

I The Wonder *(1714)*

Steele was a discriminating critic of Centlivre's plays. He praised *The Busy Body* in the *Tatler* and *The Wonder* in the *Lover*. But the four intervening plays—all produced while either the *Tatler* or the *Spectator* was being published—he passed over in silence. *The Wonder: A Woman Keeps a Secret* was produced at Drury Lane on April 27, 1714, and ran for six nights. Steele recommended it to his readers in the issue of the *Lover* published on the day of the first performance: "as we have but one British Lady who employs her Genius for the Drama, it would be a shameful Reflection on the Polite of both Sexes, should she want any Encouragement the Town can give her." As with *The Busy Body*, Steele praised Centlivre's natural abilities rather than her art. He described the "deserved Success" of *The Gamester* and *The Busy Body* as "a certain Demonstration that Wit alone is more than sufficient to supply all the Rules of Art."[1]

The central characters of *The Wonder* are the familiar two pairs of lovers: Felix and Violante, Colonel Britton and Isabella. Don Pedro intends to place his daughter Violante in a nunnery; but she is in love with Felix and means to marry him. Felix is a constant but jealous lover. Isabella is Felix's sister. Their father, Don Lopez, has contracted her to a wealthy fool, Don Gusman (an offstage character). In order to avoid this hated match, Isabella determines to run away from home. She jumps from the balcony of her room and is providentially caught by Colonel Britton. The colonel is a Scottish officer passing through Lisbon on his way home from the newly ended peninsula war. Britton carries Isabella to safety in a nearby house. It happens to be Violante's.

Isabella and Britton are soon in love. Britton is a "rover," and at first he shows some reluctance in settling down to marriage. But Isabella and her fortune together prove irresistible. The colonel's capitulation is a process of time, however. Meanwhile, Violante agrees to hide Isabella in her apartment and to keep the knowledge of her whereabouts from Felix and Don Lopez. This is the "secret" of the play's subtitle. Most of the action of the play arises from the difficulties that Violante faces in her efforts to keep it. On several occasions, circumstances make Felix suspect that Violante is unfaithful to him, while she is unable to clear herself without breaking her promise to Isabella. She must choose between her love for Felix and her loyalty to Isabella. Finally, of course, the conflict between the two is resolved—but not before Violante has been severely tested. The scenes between Felix and Violante have an emotional power unusual in Centlivre's plays. She makes us feel that Felix and Violante really do care for each other. They are the most full-blooded of Centlivre's lovers.

The subsidiary characters in *The Wonder* are the fathers and the servants. Gibby, Colonel Britton's servant, is a stereotyped stage Scotsman; his chief contribution to the play is his very broad Scottish dialect. Inis, Isabella's maid, is unremarkable. The two most amusing servants are Lissardo, Felix's man; and Flora, Violante's maid. Lissardo flirts with both maids. There is an amusing scene in Act III where he finally has to deal with both of them at once.[2] Don Pedro and Don Lopez are like the fathers in Centlivre's other plays: they are tyrannous, mercenary, and outwitted. An unusual minor character is Frederick, Felix's friend. He is outside the love relationships, but he helps the workings of the plot and sometimes serves as a mouthpiece for Centlivre's sentiments.

The Wonder is for the most part an original play. Some resemblances between *The Wonder* and George Digby's *Elvira* (c. 1663) have been noted. But the parallels are no more than the stock themes and incidents of the comedy of intrigue: concealments in closets, inopportune entries, and so on. Centlivre's only specific borrowings are from Edward Ravenscroft's *The Wrangling Lovers* (1677). She took hints from Ravenscroft for two scenes in Act IV of *The Wonder*. The reluctant parting and gradual reconciliation of Felix and Violante (pp. 51–53) recall a similar scene between Diego and Octavia in Act II of *The Wrangling Lovers*. From Act V, Octavia's difficulty in concealing both Diego and Gusman from her father is improved by Centlivre in the scene where Violante has to conceal three characters—Isabella, Felix, and Colonel Britton—from her father and from each other (pp. 48–53).[3]

If Centlivre needed a general model for *The Wonder,* she had it already in *The Perplexed Lovers.* There are enough similarities of character and incident for one to regard *The Wonder* as a greatly improved reworking of the earlier play. Felix is improved from Belvil, Violante from Camilla. Flora is developed from Florella. The scenes in which Felix unseasonably interrupts Violante recall similar incidents in *The Perplexed Lovers* with Belvil and Camilla. A clear example of both borrowing and improvement is the use in both plays of the gift of a diamond ring. In *The Perplexed Lovers,* Lord Richlove bribes Florella with a ring. She tries it on and reflects, "Odd methinks my Finger becomes a Diamond Ring as well as my Lady's" (p. 14). There the joke is dropped. In *The Wonder,* Violante rewards Lissardo for his news of Felix with a ring. Lissardo reacts in the same way as Florella: "methinks a Diamond-Ring is a vast addition to the little Finger of a Gentleman" (p. 15). But here Centlivre makes more of the incident: in the rest of the scene, the newly acquired ring makes Lissardo so proud that he will scarcely condescend to speak to Flora.

In the Preface to *The Perplexed Lovers,* Centlivre had apologized for the excesses of the Spanish plot and promised to "take Care to avoid such Absurdities for the future." In *The Wonder* she redeemed this promise. The setting is transfered from London to Lisbon, where the intrigue and business seem more natural. The plot of *The Wonder* is also more skillfully constructed: the misunderstandings are precipitated so as to involve both plot and subplot in the same web of events, and the various incidents are worked into a coherent dramatic pattern.

II *Lisbon, Love, and Liberty*

The Lisbon setting of *The Wonder* has two principal functions. Lisbon is first a more plausible locale for the comedy of intrigue. Tempers are hotter, honor more sacred, jealousy more rife than in London. Fathers and brothers exercise despotic control over their wives, daughters, and sisters. Disguise and secret assignations are accepted as everyday occurrences. Such was certainly the image of Spain and Portugal in contemporary drama. Centlivre also used the Lisbon setting to develop a contrast between English and Portuguese society and institutions. The personal and political liberty enjoyed by the English is set against the servile conditions of unenlightened despotism.

The theme is started in the first scene of the play. Don Lopez asks Frederick about the character of the English. In reply, Frederick pronounces this panegyric: "My Lord, the English are by Nature, what the ancient Romans were by Discipline[:] couragious, bold, hardy, and in love with Liberty. Liberty is the Idol of the English, under whose Banner all the Nation Lists[:] give but the Word for Liberty, and straight more armed Legions wou'd appear, than France, and Philip keep in constant Pay" (p. 2).[4] Yet there is more to this statement than the simple patriotic sentiment it appears to be. It implies that "Liberty" is sometimes no more than a political shibboleth, an "Idol" whose service is sometimes abused as a catchword or slogan. Centlivre values personal liberty, but recognizes that it too is sometimes abused as a cloak for license. This is suggested when Isabella reflects: "What pleasant Lives Women lead in England, where Duty wears no Fetter but Inclination" (p. 8).

In her treatment of the problem of parental—and by implication political—authority, Centlivre tries to work out a reasonable compromise between "Duty" and "Inclination" and between tyranny and anarchy. Don Lopez and Don Pedro both treat their daughters as their personal property, to be disposed of as they see fit. Centlivre rejects this extreme assertion of parental authority. Through Isabella, she argues that parents can expect to be obeyed only so long as their commands are reasonable. A father has no absolute authority:

Don Lopez. How, how, What do you top your second Hand Jests upon your Father, Hussy, who knows better what's good for you than you do your self; remember 'tis your Duty to Obey.
Isabella. (Rising) I never disobey'd before, and wish I had not Reason now; but Nature has got the better of my Duty, and makes me loath the harsh Commands you lay. (P. 10)

This appeal beyond "Duty" to "Reason" and "Nature" is analogous to the Whig theory of limited kingship. The family is thought of as a microcosm of the constitutional monarchy. Parents have no absolute power over their children, any more than kings have over their subjects.

Centlivre's attitude to love is as pragmatic as her treatment of liberty. She refuses to idolize or idealize either. Colonel Britton is a bluff Scot whose rakishness is reformed by the prospect of Isabella and her fortune. His attraction to Isabella is as much economic as emotional. His attitude to marriage is quite unsentimental: "I shall never be able to swallow the Matrimonial Pill, if it be not well Gilded" (p. 7). Felix is a more passionate character: his emotional involvement with Violante contrasts strongly with the colonel's prudent calculations. Their opposite temperaments illustrate the variety of love; Centlivre does not ask us to choose between them. Violante is the livelier, and Isabella the more serious, of the two heroines; but the contrast is less marked than between the two men.

Love and friendship are often at odds in the play. Centlivre uses the conflict to challenge the idea that friendship is a peculiarly male virtue. Violante's ability to keep the secret, to put Isabella's interests before her love for Felix, shows considerable strength of character: more than Felix shows when he is placed in difficulty circumstances. The play ends with Felix's admission that "thou'rt a Proof to their [women's] eternal Fame, / That Man has no Advantage but the Name" (p. 79).

That Portuguese society is inimical to both love and liberty is further illustrated by the character and situation of Frederick. There is no one corresponding to Frederick in either *The Perplexed Lovers* or *The Wrangling Lovers*. Frederick is a virtuous merchant, and he often serves as a mouthpiece for Centlivre's Whig sentiments. He is in love with Isabella, but recognizes that his case is hopeless: "a Merchant and a Grandee of Spain, are inconsistent Names" (p. 4). The attitude that excludes an eminently respectable merchant like Frederick from intermarriage with the nobility is seen as typical of Portugal's caste-ridden society. The "implied contrast," as John Loftis has observed, is "between the inflexible social structure of Portugal and the more flexible one of England."[5]

III Political Plays

Centlivre had no new play acted between *The Wonder* in April 1714 and *The Cruel Gift* in December 1716. But this gap in dramatic activity is more apparent than real. The Hanoverian succession, which Centlivre had joyfully anticipated in the Dedication to *The Wonder,* became a fact in August 1714. Centlivre celebrated it in a burst of literary activity. *A Wife Well Managed, The Gotham Election,* and *The Cruel Gift*—besides several poems—were all probably written in the second half of 1714. We know that the two farces were refused licenses by the Master of the Revels. Since Drury Lane ceased to submit plays for licensing after the grant of Steele's patent in January 1715, this can only have happened some time before that date.[6] The inference is confirmed by Centlivre's statement in her Preface that *The Gotham Election* was written "to show their Royal Highnesses the Manner of our Elections, and entertain the Town with a Subject entirely new." Evidently Centlivre had intended to capitalize on her dedication of *The Wonder* to the Duke of Cambridge. After his father's accession, he became Prince of Wales; he and his wife—"their Royal Highnesses"—arrived in England in the fall of 1714. Since an election was expected early in 1715, a play about elections would enjoy maximum topicality and appeal late in 1714. The evidence for *The Cruel Gift* having been written about the same time is the statement in its Prologue that the play was "two Winters old" and "should have courted you the last hard Frost, / But you in Ice and Politicks were lost."

The importance of establishing this chronology is that it confirms the genesis of all three plays in the political situation of 1714. It seems clear, for example, that in turning to tragedy in *The Cruel Gift,* Centlivre's motivation was as much political as literary. In the Preface to *The Gotham Election,* she singles out for praise Rowe's new play, *Lady Jane Grey.* Its production seemed to her evidence that the stage had "become a better Advocate for Protestantism than the Pulpit."

Her own tragedy—with which Rowe had assisted her—had been written as an "Advocate" for constitutional monarchy.

Centlivre's two farces were not acted, but they were published as a composite volume in 1715.[7] The Dedication—to James Craggs the younger—burns with indignation at the treatment the farces had received. Both the Dedication and the Preface are of great interest as statements of Centlivre's political feelings at the time. The strength of her anti-Catholic sentiments is worth remarking. When she speaks of the "utmost Indignation" with which she sees "those wholesome Laws neglected, which ought to be put in Execution against such profess'd Enemies of our Church and State" as the Catholic priests, we begin to wonder whether there is not an explanation of this bigotry in some biographical episode now lost. The document does not make pleasant reading, but it attests a side of Centlivre's character that should not be ignored. On its own, this virulent anti-Catholicism would account for Pope's enmity.

IV   A Wife Well Managed

This farce was refused a license because, Centlivre tells us in the Dedication, "it was said there would be Offence taken at the exposing a Popish Priest." The exposure is certainly the main point of the farce. The setting is Catholic Lisbon. Lady Pisalto hates her husband and has conceived a passion for her confessor, Father Bernardo. She confesses her love in a letter which she sends him. By ill luck—or rather through the stupidity of her Irish servant, Teague—the letter falls into the hands of her husband. Don Pisalto plots revenge on priest and wife alike. He disguises himself as Bernardo and sends his wife a letter as from the priest making an assignation. The appointment is kept, but instead of the amorous embraces Lady Pisalto is expecting she is soundly beaten. Pisalto is careful to conceal his real identity. He next contrives to send Bernardo in to his wife. The priest's own lasciviousness is exposed as, on his way, he expresses his carnal desire for Lady Pisalto.[8] He gets his just desert when Lady Pisalto and her maid thrash him in—as they suppose—revenge. Centlivre did not originate this little plot: she may have taken it either from John Dryden Jr.'s *The Husband His Own Cuckold* (1690) or from the *Heptameron*.[9]

Much of the fun of the farce is provided by the broad dialect of the Irish servant Teague. His contribution to the action is minimal: his real role in the farce is simply to speak comic Irish. A Lisbon lady with an Irish servant is surely within the license allowed to farce. The scenes of verbal comedy with Teague provide a change of pace from the main action's farce of situation and add to the variety of the play's comic effects. Centlivre had a good ear for caricaturing dialect and her plays contain a remarkable range of effects of this kind. Apart from Teague, there are several good examples: Gibby, in *The Wonder;* Num and Slouch, in *The Man's Bewitched*; and Fainwell as Jeffrey, in *The Artifice.*

V The Gotham Election

Gotham is a real place. But since at least the fifteenth century, the unfortunate village has also been "proverbial for the folly of its inhabitants."[10] In using it as the setting for her election, Centlivre was following a satirical tradition that goes back to the Towneley plays. The following is a typical joke: "There was a man of Gottam did ride to the market with two bushells on Wheate, and because his horse should beare heavy, he carried his corne upon his owne necke, & did ride upon his horse, because his horse should not carry to heavy a burthen."[11] Centlivre's electors of Gotham combine political ignorance with the grossest venality and credulity.

In 1703, Steele had been engaged on a play called *The Election of Gotham.* It was never finished, and we know no more of the play than its title. Nor is it known why Steele abandoned it; but he seems to have sold the play to John Rich and certainly became involved with Rich in a lawsuit about it. In 1713, the unfinished play was still a good stick to beat Steele with. The Tory *Examiner* pretended not to doubt that "your Author would finish his rough Draught of the Election at Goatham, according to Agreement with Mr. Rich."[12] In 1714 Steele himself used Gotham as a satirical locale in a series of papers in the *Lover.*[13] Steele and Centlivre were on friendly terms in 1714, and Steele can probably be credited with at least the title of *The Gotham Election.* Centlivre would hardly have appropriated it without his permission. Whether Steele gave her any other hints, we can only guess. Possibly he showed her his "rough Draft"—if it still existed.

The Gotham Election is primarily a political satire aimed at Tory electioneering. The subsidiary love interest is perfunctorily treated, except at the end of the play, where it is dovetailed into the political action through an allegorical betrothal scene. The venal atmosphere of Gotham and the folly of its electors are vividly created in the first two scenes. There are three candidates for the two seats that Gotham—like most parliamentary boroughs—has at Westminster. The Tory candidate is Tickup. He is a carpetbagger from London, standing for election in order to gain parliamentary immunity from arrest for debt.[14] The two Whig candidates are Sir John Worthy and Sir Roger Trusty, both local landowners. Their names are their characters: they are above the petty electioneering that Tickup descends to.

Tickup is a rascal with pro-French and Jacobite sympathies. He relies heavily on bribery and irresponsible promises, but he has also the support of two disaffected local notables. One of these is the mayor of Gotham, himself a Jacobite. The other is Lady Worthy, an extreme high church Tory. She is petulantly opposing her husband's interest as the result of a squabble they have had about the local parson. Thus Centlivre loads the scales heavily in favor of the Whigs. No man of sense would vote for Tickup. His successful canvassing of some of the electors is the index of their folly.

The political state of the borough emerges in the first scene through a conversation between Friendly and the local innkeeper, Scoredouble.[15] Friendly is in Gotham as an agent for Sir Roger Trusty. On his arrival, he learns of the mayor's daughter and her fortune and determines to win her. This intrigue is developed—and combined with the political satire—in the third scene (pp. 46–50). Friendly disguises himself as an emissary from the pretender. The mayor reveals his Jacobite sympathies and tells what he has already done in the pretender's service. The mayor is also anxious to send his daughter to be educated in France. He hopes that she will be persuaded to become a nun, so that—like Don Pedro in *The Wonder*—he can convert her fortune to his own use. Friendly offers to take her back to France with him: by this means he gets possession of the girl. He reveals her father's plot to her, and she puts herself under his protection.

There are three principal scenes of political satire: the tavern scene, the street scene, and the christening scene. The tavern scene (pp. 32–45) is a meeting of Jacobite sympathizers led by Lady Worthy and Tickup. The quality of their support is indicated by such names as Goody Gabble and Goody Shallow. Extravagant preelection promises are satirized in the series of absurd demands that Mallet makes as the price of his vote. Virtually the whole of his family must be found lucrative jobs. Tickup agrees to it all. This scene is also remarkable for some wordplay. A baker is promised the office of Master of the Rolls, and there are puns on "Patent" and on "clogs" (p. 45). Such wordplay is rare in Centlivre's plays.

The scene in the street (pp. 50–62) falls into two halves. The first half is devoted to a comic humiliation of Tickup. In order to ingratiate himself with a group of working men, Tickup sits down for a drink in the cobbler's stall. The result is that his suit is ruined and that he loses the vote: the cobbler acidly remarks that he would never vote for anyone who would "stoop so low" simply in order to buy his support (p. 54). In this scene, the political point is made through the action.

By contrast, the second half of the street scene is a serious political debate between Sir Roger Trusty and Alderman Credulous. The following exchange epitomizes the issues:

Alderman Credulous. Ay, ay, Sir Roger, we Fathers know what's good for our Children, better than they do themselves; they have nought to do but to submit to our Pleasures; Passive-Obedience is as absolutely necessary in our Wives and Children, as in Subjects to the Monarch; is not your Opinion the same, Sir Roger?
Sir Roger. Yes, whilst Husbands, Fathers and Monarchs exact nothing from us, contrary to our Religion and Laws. . . . (P. 56)

This is the same question—and in part the same words—as was argued between Isabella and Don Lopez in *The Wonder* (p. 10). In *The Gotham Election*, the mayor's tyrannical treatment of his daughter is seen as the logical corollary of his political convictions. The argument between Sir Roger and Alderman Credulous may have been expanded after Centlivre knew that the farce would not be staged. In its present form it is rather long and heavy for a farce.

After the serious debate between Sir Roger and the alderman, the play returns to Tickup. This time he visits a gathering for the christening of Mallet's grandson (pp. 62–68). Again Tickup's irresponsible promises are satirized. A new feature in this scene is the common sense view voiced by Scruple, who is a Quaker. The character of Scruple should be balanced against the satirical portrait of Prim in *A Bold Stroke for a Wife*. Centlivre carefully discriminates between them. Prim's language is more extravagant than Scruple's, and his professions less sincere.

The last scene (pp. 68–72) returns to the street. The successful candidate—not Tickup—is chaired amid a slogan-shouting mob of both parties. The disgruntled mayor threatens to declare Tickup elected despite the popular choice. At the same time, his daughter

Lucy puts herself into Friendly's hands with a speech that summarizes the convictions that Centlivre sought to express in the play:

This Day I am of Age, and I chuse you for my Guardian,—and if you can bring
me unquestionable Proofs of your being an honest Man,—that you have
always been a Lover of your Country,—a true Asserter of her Laws and
Priviledges, and that you'd spend every Shilling of my Portion in Defence of
Liberty and Property against Perkin [the Pretender] and the Pope, I'll sign,
seal, and deliver my self into your Hands the next Hour. (Pp. 69–70)

The political allegory is paramount here. Lucy (England) chooses a
guardian (George I) in preference to the father (the Pretender) who
has betrayed her.

<h2 style="text-align:center">VI   The Cruel Gift (1716)</h2>

Although Centlivre began her career with a tragedy, she soon
found comedy more congenial. By 1714, she was an experienced and
successful comic dramatist. At first sight, it seems strange that she
should turn again to tragedy after so many years. *The Cruel Gift* is
certainly a surprising development in Centlivre's career, and the
explanation probably lies in a combination of factors: ambition, her
friendship with Rowe, and her political convictions. Tragedy was
regarded as a nobler form than comedy, and ambition would naturally
prompt the comic dramatist to attempt it. Cibber, whose gifts—like
Centlivre's—were primarily comic, wrote tragedies from time to
time. The influence of Rowe is more clearly documented. Rowe
wrote the Epilogue for *The Cruel Gift,* and he also—according to
Mottley—"gave some slight Touches to the Play; particularly a Simile
of an Halcyon building her Nest in fine Weather, which ends one of
the Acts."[16] Centlivre's admiration for Rowe's political tragedies is
expressed in her Preface to *The Gotham Election. The Perjured
Husband* had no politics in it: Centlivre was following Rowe in
enlisting the stage in the service of her Whig convictions.

The Cruel Gift was produced at Drury Lane on December 17,
1716. Perhaps drawing on Centlivre's political credit with the Whigs,
it enjoyed a successful run of six nights. There was a seventh
performance on May 3, 1717—by royal command and for Centlivre's
benefit—but the play was not subsequently revived. Yet the popularity of *The Cruel Gift* was not entirely political in origin. A hostile
contemporary pamphlet grudgingly admitted that it "won the Town's
Applause."[17] Especially when it is considered as the work of a comic

dramatist, *The Cruel Gift* is a very respectable performance. It is certainly Centlivre's most successfully sustained serious play, and the level of the verse is higher than she achieved elsewhere in either her plays or her poems.

The Cruel Gift is set in Verona, at the court of the king of Lombardy. The king's daughter (Leonora) has secretly married a military hero (Lorenzo), who is not, however, of royal blood. The king is expected to disapprove strongly of the match. Lorenzo is the son of a former prime minister (Alcanor, now deceased). The present prime minister (Antenor) is a long-time rival of Alcanor and therefore an enemy to Lorenzo. In addition, Antenor had ambitiously intended that his own son (Learchus) should marry Leonora. Learchus does not share his father's ambitions: instead, he is in love with Lorenzo's sister (Antimora). Lorenzo wants Antimora to marry his friend Cardono, but Antimora is in love with Learchus and refuses to do so. This tangled complex of rivalries and relationships develops into a series of conflicts between the claims of love and duty. Leonora is torn between her duty to her father and her love for Lorenzo. Learchus has to set loyalty to his father against his love for Antimora. Antimora in turn has to choose between her duty to her brother and her love for Learchus.

In *The Perjured Husband,* Bassino was likewise torn between love and duty, but in that play the conflicts were only argued in debates. In *The Cruel Gift,* the questions are debated, but the conflicts of loyalty also develop into real choices that have to be made in the context of the turbulent political state of Lombardy. The tragedy is not abstract and disembodied, as it was in *The Perjured Husband.* Personal loyalties are complicated by political ones: personal choices have more immediate and more far-reaching consequences.

The plot develops from Antenor's discovery of the relationship between Leonora and Lorenzo. Ambition and revenge lead him to reveal it to the king, who is enraged and determines to punish the guilty lovers. Lorenzo is seized and condemned to death. But since Lorenzo is popular with the common people, there is an uprising in his favor. The revolt is crushed, however, and it falls to Learchus to carry out the king's sentence of death. Lorenzo's heart is to be ripped out and sent to Leonora in a goblet. There is a major emotional scene when Leonora receives the goblet and the news of Lorenzo's death.[18] Her stoic fortitude under the blow moves the king to repent his cruel revenge on Lorenzo.

A happy ending is contrived through the subplot. When Lorenzo is first imprisoned, Antimora asks Learchus to free her brother. Learchus hesitates to disobey the king. In a classic example of "heroic" behavior, Antimora puts her duty to her brother before her love for Learchus. She offers to marry Cardono—whom she hates—if he will secure her brother's freedom. At this point, the intrigues and the sequence of events become involved. The end result of the plots and counterplots is that Antenor is killed while suppressing the popular uprising and Cardono is killed in an attempt to rescue Lorenzo. Learchus delays the execution of Lorenzo and sends a substitute heart to Leonora. The king's subsequent repentance confirms the wisdom of Learchus's initiative. The reconciliation between the king and his daughter and son-in-law is completed by an unexpected development. A hermit arrives at the court: he reveals that he is the long-lost deposed duke of Milan and that Lorenzo is his son—not Alcanor's as had been thought.[19] The king now accepts Lorenzo as a suitable match for his daughter, and the royal lovers are united. The union of Learchus and Antimora is likewise foreshadowed.

Centlivre's sources for the main plot of *The Cruel Gift* were the first tale of the fourth day in Boccaccio's *Decameron* and Dryden's rendering of the story in his *Fables, Ancient and Modern* (1700).[20] In both Boccaccio and Dryden, the lover is really murdered, and the princess poisons herself. Centlivre's chief alterations to the story are the happy ending, the secret of Lorenzo's birth, and the addition of the Learchus-Antimora subplot. The political themes and the characterization are also Centlivre's own.

Perhaps the least satisfactory element in the play is the management of the catastrophe. Learchus's substitution of the heart, and Lorenzo's survival, come as a complete surprise to the audience. This is obviously necessary in order to avoid undercutting the force of Leonora's great scene, but when the news is broken, the result is too abrupt a change of mood and feeling. Such surprises were, however, admired by some contemporaries. John Dennis complained about Addison's *Cato* that "here then are none of those beautiful Surprizes which are to be found in some of the Grecian Tragedies, and in some of our own." Dennis thought it impossible that either pity or terror could be "excited in a very great Degree, without a very great Surprize."[21] But even if we accept the surprise as a conscious effect, the device of the hermit is surely a clumsy one.

The Cruel Gift is not a very affecting tragedy. The characters fail to engage our interest, and the plot appears contrived. Centlivre's pathos is inferior to Rowe's. But the play is still a distinct advance in technique on *The Perjured Husband*. In the Prologue, George Sewell calls *The Cruel Gift* "her first Attempt in Tragick-Stuff." Perhaps he chose to disregard *The Perjured Husband* as a hybrid form. There is no mixture of styles or genres in *The Cruel Gift*: there is no comic subplot, and it is written entirely in verse.

An interesting contemporary discussion of tragedy is Addison's paper in the *Spectator* (No. 40). Addison allows tragedy to end either happily or unhappily, as appropriate. But he condemns both tragicomedy and—in general—tragedies that have double plots. Addison follows Dryden, however, in allowing some latitude in the matter of subplots. He allows that the "Inconvenience" of dividing the interest of the audience between two actions "may in a great Measure be cur'd, if not wholly remov'd, by the skilful Choice of an Under-Plot, which may bear such a near Relation to the principal Design, as to contribute towards the Completion of it, and be concluded by the same Catastrophe."[22] In *The Cruel Gift*, both plots turn on the same action: Learchus's reprieve of Lorenzo. In addition, the two plots certainly have a "near Relation" to each other both in theme and action.

There are no political implications in the story as Boccaccio tells it in the *Decameron*. In the *Fables*, Dryden described the king as having "turn'd a Tyrant in his latter Days," but did not develop the theme of tyranny any further in the poem.[23] Centlivre, on the other hand, makes a good deal of the political situations and events in the play. *The Cruel Gift* contains a number of indirect allusions to public affairs in England. The king is the mayor of Gotham writ large, a would-be absolute monarch. His authoritarian attitude to Leonora is consistent with his general absolutist principles. In the first scene of the play, the king's capricious and arbitrary behavior is contrasted with Learchus's unexceptionably Whig sentiments. Learchus professes himself willing to fight any enemy of his country, but refuses to be a party to any attempt to suppress liberty at home:

> But he who would enslave his native Land,
> Give up the reverend Rights of Law and Justice,
> To the detested Lust of boundless Tyranny,
> Pollute our Altars, change our holy Worship,
> Deserves the Curses both of Heaven and Earth. (P. 3)

This speech has obvious reference to the Jacobite plots—and in 1715 the actual rebellion—to restore "James III" and to reestablish the

Catholic religion in England. During the course of the play, Learchus's loyalty to the king is seriously strained by the king's order to execute Lorenzo. This order is both unjust and arbitrary. Learchus's refusal to carry it out shows that he recognizes a higher authority than the king's.

The king never explicitly renounces his absolutist principles, but at the end of the play he is much chastened. The death of Antenor provides a convenient scapegoat, and there is a promise of a more responsible exercise of royal power in future. Contemporaries might have seen in the wily Antenor a caricature of the Earl of Oxford, Lord Treasurer in the Tory government of 1710 to 1714. Likewise, the king's ingratitude to Lorenzo could be taken as a reference to the Duke of Marlborough's loss of court favor. The scene at the beginning of Act II (pp. 16–18), in which the ambassadors from Tuscany are summarily dismissed, reflects Centlivre's bellicose attitude to the war and her dissatisfaction with the terms of the Peace of Utrecht. Writing *The Cruel Gift* in the latter part of 1714, it would be natural for Centlivre to incorporate such references into the political situations in her tragedy. But the play is not a political allegory, and it is difficult to be certain about the interpretation of possible allusions to particular people and events.

What is clear is the general political tenor of *The Cruel Gift*. It celebrates personal and political liberty. John Loftis has shown that such "tragedies celebrating the limitation of royal power, of constitutional monarchy as conceived by Locke" were "abundant after the Revolution." But *The Cruel Gift* is largely free of the "exaggerated earnestness, over-emphatic statement, and over-simplified argument" that Loftis finds to be characteristic of the type.[24] This is the result of Centlivre's tactful subordination of the political to the personal. *The Cruel Gift* is first of all a tragedy of conflicting loyalties; only secondarily is it an indictment of royal absolutism.

CHAPTER 7

A Bold Stroke for a Wife
and The Artifice

THE earlier part of Centlivre's career is characterized by a
tendency to repeat the same dramatic formula. *The Beau's Duel,
Love's Contrivance,* and *Love at a Venture,* for example, are all
variations on the same basic pattern. *The Wonder* is essentially an
improved reworking of *The Perplexed Lovers.* But after *The Wonder,*
Centlivre ceased to repeat herself. Her last five plays are quite
different from each other and from her earlier work. The range of
these later plays is remarkable. Nor is the variety of these plays
simply a question of genre: the contrast between the last two
comedies is hardly less than that between *The Cruel Gift* and the two
farces.

I   A Bold Stroke for a Wife *(1718)*

A Bold Stroke for a Wife is the third and last of Centlivre's major
comedies. It was produced at Lincoln's Inn Fields on February 3,
1718, and ran for six nights. It ranks as one of Centlivre's best plays
because of the way a variety of comic effects is worked into a coherent
unity. Alone of Centlivre's full length plays, it has no subplot. Yet it
has as much variety as any of Centlivre's multiple plot plays. Colonel
Fainwell and Ann Lovely have agreed on marriage before the play
begins. But Anne recognizes that "love makes but a slovenly figure in
that house where poverty keeps the door."[1] Fainwell has only his
pay, and Anne's fortune has been left to her on condition that she
marry with the consent of her guardians. The whole action of the play
is concerned with tricking the four guardians into giving their consent
to Fainwell's marrying Anne.

The difficulty of the task—and the source of the play's comic
variety—is that Anne's father chose a quartet of guardians who seem
108

unlikely to agree about anything: a beau, an antiquary, a stockjobber, and a Quaker. Each of the guardians is determined to approve only a husband of his own kind for Anne. In order to gain their consents, Fainwell has to assume a series of disguises. One of them fails to do the trick, so that he puts on five different ones altogether: as a man of fashion, as a learned traveler, as a country steward, as a Dutch merchant, and as a Quaker. In earlier Centlivre comedies, eccentric humor characters were often introduced without being well integrated into the play. In *A Bold Stroke for a Wife,* the odd humors of the guardians—and the corresponding characters that Fainwell assumes to humor them—are central to the comedy. The comedy of humors is perfectly dovetailed into the love plot: the same comic business serves to illustrate the humor and to advance the plot.

The originality of *A Bold Stroke for a Wife* is emphasized in both the Dedication and the Prologue. In the Dedication, Centlivre claims that "the plot is entirely new and the incidents wholly owing to my own invention, not borrowed from our own or translated from the works of any foreign poet" (p. 5). The unidentified "Gentleman" who wrote the Prologue makes a similar claim:

> Tonight we come upon a bold design,
> To try to please without one borrowed line.
> Our plot is new, and regularly clear,
> And not one single tittle from Molière.
> O'er buried poets we with caution tread,
> And parish sextons leave to rob the dead. (P. 6)

But these protestations cannot be taken at their face value.

In the account of Centlivre in his *List of All the English Dramatic Poets* (1747), Mottley wrote of *A Bold Stroke for a Wife:* "In this Play she was assisted by Mr. Mottley, who wrote one or two entire Scenes of it."[2] This claim is hard to assess. Mottley was a clerk in the Excise Office in 1718. Perhaps he put his familiarity with the workings of the city—and possibly a knowledge of Dutch—to use in the scenes in Jonathan's coffeehouse. But these scenes do not stand out in style. But whatever her debt to Mottley, Centlivre's claim of complete originality is suspect on other grounds. There are some parallels with earlier plays that are too close to be regarded as coincidences.

We need not look for specific sources for such stock themes and devices as satire on Quaker hypocrisy or antiquarianism or the use of disguises to trick parents or guardians. But there are some interesting parallels of incident with Abraham Cowley's *Cutter of Coleman Street* (1661) and Dryden's *Sir Martin Mar-All* (1667).[3] Nor was a plot based on the idea of outwitting guardians of opposite humors new. In Thomas Dilke's *The Lover's Luck* (1696), the heroine (Mrs. Purflew) has two guardians: Sir Nicholas Purflew, " a formal Herald and Antiquary"; and Alderman Whim, "a Projector and Humorist." The alderman supports the suit of Breviat, a lawyer; Sir Nicholas prefers Goosandelo, a fop. Mrs. Purflew is actually won by the man she loves, Colonel Bellair. If Centlivre did not know this play, the resemblance of plot between it and *A Bold Stroke for A Wife* is a remarkable coincidence.

It is often difficult to draw a firm line between specific borrowings and the use by different authors of the same stock device. A case in point is the incident (in Act V) of the two Simon Pures. Obadiah Prim is the last of the guardians to be tricked. Fainwell impersonates Simon Pure, a Quaker whom Prim is expecting from Bristol. Fainwell does very well until the inopportune arrival of the real Simon Pure. John Genest thought that this incident was borrowed from Newburgh Hamilton's farce *The Petticoat Plotter* (1712, but not printed until 1720).[4] But Centlivre's incident is so much more elaborate than Hamilton's that it is difficult to think of the latter as a source.

In any case, the idea did not originate with Hamilton. There are similar incidents in *Cutter of Coleman Street* and in Cibber's *She Would and She Would Not* (1702). In Act V of *Cutter of Coleman Street*, Worm and Puny impersonate Jolly's long-lost brother and the brother's servant. William and Ralph, two of Jolly's servants, assume identical disguises in order to test the new arrivals. Worm and Puny are discomfited by the arrival of the "real" brother and sneak away. Closer to the incident in *A Bold Stroke for A Wife* is Hypolita's impersonation of Don Philip in *She Would and She Would Not*. Hypolita successfully imposes on Don Manuel, and when the real Don Philip arrives, she is able to convince Don Manuel that he is the imposter. So too, Fainwell manages to convince Prim that he is the real Simon Pure. If Centlivre took hints from Cowley or Cibber, she improved them considerably. In Cibber the deception is spread over several scenes, and it is aided by the theft of Don Philip's papers. Centlivre improves the comic effect by compressing the incident into a single scene. In addition, Fainwell's deception depends entirely on his verbal skill. He has no stolen papers to help him out. He convinces Prim that he is the real Simon Pure because he can imitate the Quaker idiom more convincingly than Pure can speak it.

Other similar incidents could be cited: the impersonation of Vincentio in *The Taming of the Shrew*, for example. Yet it is probably best to regard the Simon Pure episode as a reworking of a common comic device rather than a direct borrowing from any one source. Centlivre's claim of complete originality in *A Bold Stroke for A Wife* is an overstatement, but she certainly improved what she borrowed from the common stock of comedy.

II *The Guardians*

In selecting follies and humors to satirize in the characters of the four eccentric guardians, Centlivre avoided what must have been a temptation to make them all Tory types. Instead, she chose her targets from both parties. In the list of characters, the guardians are described as follows: Sir Philip Modelove as "an old beau"; Periwinkle as "a kind of silly virtuoso"; Tradelove as "a change-broker"; and Obadiah Prim as "a Quaker" (p. 8). Sir Philip and Periwinkle are conservatives, Tories in sympathy, and lovers and admirers of the past. Tradelove and Prim—who is a glover by trade as well as a Quaker—represent the newer, forward-looking, Whiggish mercantile classes. Thus the satire is evenly distributed.

Sir Philip and Prim represent opposite extremes of the moral and social spectrums. Sir Philip is a beau and a libertine, but there is a hint (p. 22) that his professed libertinism is only a show. Prim's rigid morality, by contrast, conceals his lasciviousness. When he takes exception to Anne's décolletage, she reminds him that "you had no aversion to naked bosoms when you begged [Mary, his servant] to show you a little, little, little bit of her delicious bubby" (p. 31). Mrs. Prim's sexual hypocrisy is also exposed later in the play (p. 76). Such satire on Quaker hypocrisy was a common dramatic theme.[5]

Sir Philip also belongs to a well-known stage type. He affects French words, dress, and manners. Nor is he an originator, but rather an imitator of fashionable follies. Thus he belongs to the tradition of Sir Fopling Flutter in *The Man of Mode* (1676) rather than to the type of the original fop, such as Sir Novelty Fashion in *Love's Last Shift* (1696). There are several such fops in Centlivre's earlier plays: Sir William Mode in *The Beau's Duel*, for example. Sir Philip differs from them in both character and role. He is not actively in pursuit of any woman, and his characteristic manner is an affected languid indifference. His indolence is that of the supine voluptuary: "I had the offer of a barony about five years ago, but I abhorred the fatigue which must have attended it. I could never yet bring myself to join with either party" (p. 22). Despite the last disclaimer, the reference fixes Sir Philip as a Tory. The oblique allusion is to the creation of twelve new Tory peers in 1712. Centlivre implies that some of the peers who were created were even less qualified to be legislators than Sir Philip.

If beaus and Quakers were familiar satiric butts, so were antiquaries and stockjobbers. Periwinkle is both a collector of the rubbish of antiquity and a credulous student of natural history. He has more in common with Fossile in the Gay-Pope-Arbuthnot *Three Hours After Marriage* (1717) than with Sir Nicholas Gimcrack in Shadwell's *The Virtuoso* (1676). It is clear from the sympathetic portrait of Valeria in *The Basset Table* that Centlivre saw nothing absurd in experimental science. But she could laugh readily enough at any uncritical reverence for the past. A notable Tory who had antiquarian interests was the Earl of Oxford. Steele satirized him in the character of Sir Anthony Crabtree in the *Lover* (1714). In one paper, Sir Anthony is reported to be planning to sell his collection, which includes an Egyptian mummy and wax used by John of Gaunt.[6]

Even Tories, however, could ridicule credulous collectors of spurious antiquities. The three doctors in *Three Hours after Marriage* reach a crescendo of absurdity:

Fossile. Your haft of the antediluvian trowel, unquestionably the tool of one of the Babel masons!
Nautilus. What's that to your fragment of Seth's pillar?
Possum. Gentleman, I affirm that I have a greater curiosity than all of them. I have an entire leaf of Noah's journal aboard the ark, that was hewen out of a porphyry pillar in Palmyra.[7]

Among the rarities that Fainwell claims to possess are "an Egyptian's idol," "two pair of Chinese nutcrakers," "a muff made from the feathers of those geese that saved the Roman Capitol" (pp. 40, 42). Centlivre's satire is less imaginative than that in *Three Hours after Marriage*. Periwinkle prides himself on a coat "that was formerly worn by that ingenious and very learned person John Tradescant" (p. 39). Fainwell's rarities are scarcely exaggerated examples that could almost have been drawn from the collections of the real Tradescant. These included "Two feathers of the Phoenix tayle"; "A piece of Stone of Saint John Baptists Tombe"; and "Edward the Confessors knit-gloves."[8]

Tradelove's world is centered on Exchange Alley and Jonathan's coffeehouse, where every scrap of news and rumor is sought after for its likely effect on stock prices. Fainwell invented rarities for Periwinkle; he invents a rumor for Tradelove. Stockjobbers like Tradelove were regularly attacked by both Tory and Whig sympathizers. But John Loftis points out that Whig dramatists particularly were careful to "distinguish between merchants and stockjobbers, portraying the one sympathetically and the other satirically."[9] Merchants increased the wealth of the country; stockjobbers were financial parasites. In *A Bold Stroke for a Wife*, Centlivre draws a contrast between Tradelove and Freeman, a genuine merchant and Fainwell's friend. Like Frederick in *The Wonder*, Freeman shows that merchants can be useful and virtuous members of society.

In *The Anatomy of Exchange Alley* (1719), Daniel Defoe describes stockjobbing as "a Trade founded in Fraud, born of Deceit, and nourished by" such tricks as "Coining false News."[10] In William Taverner's comedy *The Female Advocates* (1713), there is an unscrupulous financier called Sir Charles Transfer. His character lends point to the following rhetorical climax: "Rot your Money . . . I'll Beg first, Rob on the High-way, or turn Stock-Jobber and cheat all the World."[11]

Thus all four of the guardians have their counterparts in contemporary satire and drama. Centlivre was drawing on stock types that would be immediately recognized as satirical butts. Yet the total effect of *A Bold Stroke for a Wife* is comic rather than satiric. The guardians are not very harshly treated. Thalia Stathas sees them as transitional figures: although they "cannot evoke the affectionate laughter accorded to eccentrics in later eighteenth-century literature . . . they are not the targets for merciless ridicule that they would have been in most earlier comedy."[12] Sir Philip, Prim, and Periwinkle are more self-deceived than deceivers of others. Only Tradelove is an actively malevolent character, and Centlivre treats him more harshly than the others.

III   *The Action*

The principal comic effects in *A Bold Stroke for a Wife* are disguise and deception. Because of the repeated use of the same basic device—Fainwell's outwitting each guardian in turn by assuming an appropriate character—Centlivre had to be particularly careful to prevent the repetition becoming too apparent. The problem was partly solved by the very different characters of the guardians: we are less aware of the repetition, since each is attacked in a different way. But Centlivre also made each successive guardian more difficult to outwit, and varied the pace and structure of each act. By these means, the comedy's momentum is maintained and the tension increased toward the climax in Act V.

After an initial act of exposition, each succeeding act is concerned with one of the guardians. But no two acts follow the same pattern. The disposition of scenes is as follows:

Act I. Scene i: Tavern. Fainwell and allies.
    Scene ii: Prim's. Anne.

Act II. Scene i: the Park. Outwitting Sir Philip.
    Scene ii: Prim's. First general meeting of the guardians.

Act III. Tavern. Unsuccessful attempt to trick Periwinkle.

Act IV. Scene i: Jonathan's. The plot against Tradelove begun.
    Scene ii: Tavern. The plot against Tradelove continued.
    Scene iii: Periwinkle's. Successful second attempt to trick Periwinkle.
    Scene iv: Tavern. The plot against Tradelove concluded.

Act V. Prim's. The last trick, the Simon Pure episode, and the final gathering of the guardians.

It will be seen from the above that unity of action does not preclude variety of plotting.

Act II opens Fainwell's campaign on a low key note. The indolent and amiable Sir Philip is easily deceived by Fainwell in the character of a fop. In Scene ii, Sir Philip introduces Fainwell—still in his assumed role—to the other guardians, who have assembled at Prim's. Needless to say, the others reject him as a suitable husband for Anne. The function of this scene is to provide a pause in the action and to introduce the remaining characters. Bringing the guardians together thus early in the play serves to emphasize their incompatibility and the difficulty of Fainwell's task.

Act III is occupied by an unsuccessful attempt to gull Periwinkle. It was enough for Fainwell to act the fop in order to win over the easygoing Sir Philip; Periwinkle is not so easily taken in. Fainwell assumes the guise of a learned traveler who has collected many rarities. The act moves from comedy to farce as the rarities that Fainwell describes become more and more extravagant. The height of absurdity is reached with the pretended girdle of invisibility. The use of this wonder is demonstrated by means of a convenient trapdoor, and Periwinkle agrees to exchange his consent to Anne's marriage for possession of the girdle. The illusion is unluckily punctured just too soon by the entry of one of the tavern waiters, who addresses Fainwell as "Colonel."

This act is the weakest in the play. The trapdoor and the waiter's interruption are both clumsy devices, and the account of Fainwell's rarities (pp. 38–43) is overlong. The weakness stands out in comparison with the similar scenes in *Three Hours after Marriage*. There the antiquarian satire—of which a sample was quoted above—is more compressed and more pointed. The comedy that derives from Plotwell's "touch-stone of virginity" is also managed more adroitly than Fainwell's business with the girdle of invisibility.

By contrast with the single scene of Act III, Act IV is divided into four scenes. The plot becomes more involved, and it begins to move faster. The atmosphere of frenzied stockjobbing and rumor-mongering is set in the first scene. Fainwell is disguised as a Dutch merchant, and the duping of Tradelove is effected through the coordinated plan of Fainwell and Freeman. Their plot is prepared and executed with military precision. Tradelove is hooked with a bait of false "news" and lays a wager with Fainwell on the strength of it. When he discovers that the "news" is false, he gives his consent in exchange for canceling the wager.

In Scene iii, the plot against Tradelove is interrupted by a second attempt on Periwinkle. This time Fainwell pretends to be the steward of Periwinkle's uncle, bringing "news" of the uncle's death. The use of false "news" provides a thematic link with the duping of Tradelove. In the excitement of this unexpected inheritance, Periwinkle signs what he takes to be a lease, but which is actually a form of consent to Fainwell's marrying Anne. Fainwell leaves Periwinkle to his grandiose dreams of amassing a great collection and founding a museum.

The pattern is again varied in Act V. The act begins with a second gathering of the guardians; but the promise of a speedy resolution proves premature and they disperse. The tension picks up again as Fainwell arrives disguised as Simon Pure. This is his most daring trick, for Pure is not only a real person but is known to be on his way to Prim's. Fainwell is now working against the clock, as well as the guardian, for the first time in the play. His intrigue prospers until the arrival of the real Simon Pure. But in a grand scene of competing Quaker rhetoric, the real Pure is routed. He retires to secure proof of his identity. The pace quickens and the tension mounts. Two lines before Pure's return (p. 93), Prim signs the vital form, and Fainwell and Anne are safe.

The guardians are all assembled for the last time. Each in turn is discomfited, as Fainwell reveals the sequence of his tricks and disguises. Finally he reassumes his true character and identity— something we have almost forgotten—as a British soldier: "I have had the honor to serve his Majesty and headed a regiment of the bravest fellows that every pushed bayonet in the throat of a Frenchman; and . . . whenever my country wants my aid, this sword and arm are at her service" (p. 98). Thus the comedy ends on a popular patriotic note.

Despite its prominent farcical episodes—notably in Act III—*A Bold Stroke for a Wife* is a serious comedy. Through the characters of the guardians, Centlivre presents a group of social antitypes. Centlivre's satire is directed less at the occupational groups which they represent than at narrowmindedness and social intolerance in general. Centlivre argues by implication for a broadly tolerant mixed society in which individuals are free to follow their own bents—she does not want to "reform" the guardians in any way—but in which fashion, learning, business, and religion are not so far apart that they cannot meet on common ground. In such a society, no guardian would seek to impose a man of his own kind on Anne or to prevent her marrying a suitable husband of her own choice.

IV   The Artifice *(1722)*

Although not produced until late in 1722, *The Artifice* was probably written about three years earlier. On February 20, 1720, the *Weekly Packet* published a report that *The Artifice* would "shortly be acted" at Drury Lane.[13] The reasons for the long delay are not known, but other authors suffered similar treatment from the managers of Drury Lane. A comedy by Mary Manley—*The Double Mistress: or, 'Tis Well 'Tis No Worse*—was also announced in the *Weekly Packet* on February 20: it seems never to have been performed. A few months earlier, John Dennis had complained, in the Dedication to *The Invader of his Country* (1719), that this play had been long delayed for no good reason and then finally produced at an unfavorable moment. Dennis further charged that the Drury Lane managers were in general hostile to new plays. Dennis argued that the managers' shortsighted pursuit of a crassly commercial policy—producing "the most Absurd and Insipid Trifles that ever came upon any Stage" in preference to his own tragedy—would result in the eventual ruin of the theater and the decline of the drama.[14]

The Artifice received some complimentary notice just before it was produced, on September 22, 1722, in the *St. James's Journal* and in the *Freeholder's Journal* on September 26. But these attempts to excite interest in the new play had little result. *The Artifice* opened at Drury Lane on October 2 but ran for only three nights. It was the first of Centlivre's acted plays since *The Perplexed Lovers* in 1712 not to reach the common standard of dramatic success, a sixth night and a second benefit.

The Artifice contains some incidential topical satire which gave offense in certain quarters. But this was probably not the decisive factor in the play's failure. We need look no further than the play itself for reasons for its lack of success. *The Artifice* is Centlivre's longest play: the first edition runs to one hundred six pages of text. If it was indeed produced in its entirety, its sheer length may have resulted in tedium. The plot is both complicated and slow-moving, and there are several long, static scenes. Nor is *The Artifice* a coherent play: it moves from farce close to tragedy and from the salacious to the sentimental. Scenes of buffoonery follow scenes of serious emotional content. The parts of the play are indulged to the detriment of the whole.

There can, however, be no doubt that these effects are the result of conscious artistic choice rather than failure of technique. Centlivre had just shown, in *A Bold Stroke for a Wife*, that she could write a well-constructed comedy observing unity of action. In *The Artifice*, she chose to return to the earlier pattern of her multiple plot comedies. Some parts of the play are actually reminiscent of her earlier comedies. The main action of *The Artifice* recalls *The Beau's Duel*. In *The Artifice*, the mercenary father is Sir Philip Moneylove. He approved of Sir John Freeman as a suitor for his daughter Olivia, until Sir John was disinherited in favor of his younger brother Ned. Sir Philip now insists that Olivia should marry Ned. Olivia, of course, remains faithful to Sir John.

Ned Freeman, a peripheral figure in the nominal main plot, is at the center of the second and third plots. Ned was previously betrothed to a Dutch girl (Louisa), and according to the Dutch custom, the exchange of solemn promises was followed by consummation of the "marriage." Louisa is now the mother of Ned's child. But since inheriting the estate, Ned has repudiated and abandoned Louisa on the pretext that no ceremony was performed. He is now in search of an heiress and wants to marry Olivia. Louisa, however, aided by Sir John and Olivia, arrives in London and tricks Ned into marrying her and resigning the estate to Sir John. As a palliative, Louisa reveals that since her father's death, she has been in possession of a fortune of £40,000. Ned is now satisfied.

Quite independently of these serious involvements with Louisa and Olivia, Ned carries on a cuckolding intrigue with Mrs. Watchit. She is young and lively, her husband old and jealous. This plot is like Bellair's intrigue with Lady Cautious in *Love at a Venture*. Ned does not quite succeed in cuckolding Watchit. Some good comes of the intrigue, for it teaches Mrs. Watchit and her husband valuable moral lessons. On sober reflection, Mrs. Watchit is glad to have preserved—albeit accidentally—her virtue. At the end of the play, she and her husband are reconciled on much the same terms as Sir Paul and Lady Cautious. Watchit admits that he has been unreasonably jealous and promises to be so no longer. In return, Mrs. Watchit promises fidelity and complaisance for the future.

The fourth plot concerns Ensign Fainwell's campaign to trick the wealthy Widow Headless into marriage. Fainwell's weapon in this campaign is disguise. His attacks on the widow involve two assumed identities, as a rustic servant (Jeffrey) and as a country squire (Mr. Worthy). This plot is loosely connected with the rest of the play through Sir Philip Moneylove. In return for a share in the widow's fortune, Sir Philip has introduced an adventurer (Tally) to her under the name of Lord Pharoah-Bank. This imposture plays on one of the widow's humors—her determination to marry only a lord. Her other humor is her eccentric attitude to servants: she prefers them straight from the country so that she can bully, scold, and "polish" them.

In other plays, Centlivre successfully used serious and comic actions to counterpoint each other. But in *The Artifice* there is no consistent pattern of contrasts: the raw incongruities are simply juxtaposed. Centlivre provides no coherent moral perspective for the play as a whole. In the struggle for Olivia, Centlivre directs our sympathies toward Sir John. In the affair with Louisa, Ned is again the villain. Yet in his intrigue with Mrs. Watchit, Ned is an engaging and attractive figure. Centlivre portrays him more sympathetically than the jealous old husband. It is the same Ned—unprincipled, selfish, and heartless—but the moral viewpoint varies. The problem is not inconsistency of characterization, but confusion of values. Sir Philip's mercenary attitude to his daughter's marriage is condemned.

Yet exactly the same philosophy is approved in Fainwell's wooing of the widow.

The failure to apply a consistent moral standard also makes the reformation of Ned Freeman less convincing than the similar reformations of Valere in *The Gamester* and Charles Gripe in *Marplot*. In the earlier plays, the process of contrition was begun in response to an exemplary moral action. In *The Gamester*, it was Angelica's generous forgiveness of Valere's loss of the picture. In *Marplot*, it was Isabinda's rescue of Charles from Don Perriera despite his infidelity to her. But in *The Artifice*, Louisa fails to achieve a comparable moral standing. Instead of convincing Ned by her own behavior of the error of his ways, she tricks him into marrying her. The moral point of Ned's change of heart is thereby weakened.

The most amusing part of *The Artifice* is Ned's intrigue with Mrs. Watchit. Yet even here there is a falling off in comic power compared with Centlivre's earlier plays. The weakness of the comedy is evident even in the "screen" scene which is one of the play's highlights. [15] This scene is a variant on one of Centlivre's favorite incidents: a young man inconveniently discovered in a lady's apartment. There is such a scene in most of Centlivre's comedies. In *The Artifice,* Ned makes and keeps an assignation with Mrs. Watchit. The pair are about to retire to her bedroom when Watchit returns unexpectedly. There is only sufficient warning for Ned to hide behind a screen. Mrs. Watchit tries to engross her husband's attention so that Ned can slip out. Ned tries to back out but is observed by Watchit. Impudently enough, Ned pretends that he has just come in and takes the offensive against Watchit for not having servants to answer the bell. The structure of the scene—especially the effective reversal after Watchit sees Ned—is good, but the scene itself is too long and slow moving. Centlivre's sense of dramatic economy—evident in the similar "hood" scene in *The Wonder* (pp. 53–54)—failed her in this instance.

The Artifice, then, is a disappointing play. It is too long, and Centlivre tried to pack into it too many different actions and effects without sufficiently considering the resulting incongruities of tone and inconsistency of morality. The serious plot is weakened by turning on an "artifice" rather than an exemplary action. In fact, *The Artifice* really contains the raw material for two plays. The struggle between Sir John and Ned for Olivia and the family estate, combined with Louisa's attempt to reclaim Ned for herself, would have made a serious comedy of the same kind as Cibber's *Love's Last Shift* (1696) and Farquhar's *The Twin Rivals* (1702). The play could have been balanced by lighter comedy of one kind or another, perhaps by making Sir Philip a more humorous character.

A second play—resembling Centlivre's own *Love at a Venture*— could have been made out of Ned's intrigue with Mrs. Watchit and Fainwell's courting of the widow. It would only be necessary to add a seriously presented heroine whom Ned would finally have married. The result would have been a lighthearted comedy of intrigue untroubled by moral earnestness. By thus dividing up the material of *The Artifice*, Centlivre could have created two very different comedies, each a coherent unity.

V   *Politics and Parnassus*

A detailed attack on *The Artifice* was published in the *Monthly Packet of Advices from Parnassus* in November 1722.[16] Although its criticism is largely a pretext for an attack on Centlivre's politics, the paucity of any kind of contemporary commentary on Centlivre's plays makes even such an attack of some critical interest. The *Monthly Packet's* remarks do not much illuminate *The Artifice* itself—which the author at times willfully misrepresents—but they do afford evidence of how at least one contemporary reacted to the play. The views expressed in the *Monthly Packet* are perhaps typical of the hostile reception that Centlivre's politics would guarantee her plays among the Tories, the Catholics, and the Jacobites.

One of the major political events of 1722 was the discovery of a Jacobite plot to restore the Stuart dynasty. The bishop of Rochester, Francis Atterbury, was the most prominent public figure implicated in the plot. Atterbury's Jacobite sympathies had long been common knowledge. He was arrested in August 1722 and imprisoned in the Tower of London. His trial occasioned a flow of polemical pamphlets and also provoked public demonstrations against the Jacobites and the Non-Jurors.

The Artifice contains a number of topical hits at the Non-Jurors and the Catholics. Sir John Freeman is a staunch Whig, but his father had been a Jacobite. Sir John was disinherited after the following escapade came to his father's knowledge: "One Day, in my Cups, I chanced to stumble into a Non-juring-Meeting, with half a Dozen honest Officers at my Back, drove out the Congregation, ty'd the Parson Neck and Heels, lock'd the Door, and took the Key in my Pocket" (p. 5). The *Monthly Packet* asks whether Centlivre thought this episode "a piece of good Manners, good Breeding, or Fortitude."[17] Surely Centlivre could have found a better pretext for disinheriting Sir John: an incident that would have been in character without making a partisan political point.

Another intrusive satirical point is made against the toleration of Catholic priests. Mrs. Watchit is made a Catholic for this sole purpose. In an incident that may be derived from Boccaccio—it is found in the fifth tale of the seventh day in the *Decameron*—Watchit impersonates his wife's confessor in order to discover the secret affair that he suspects she is conducting. But his ruse is discovered, and Mrs. Watchit—like the wife in the *Decameron*—turns the tables on her husband. The incident serves to introduce satirical reflections on the Catholic clergy. The same theme is continued later in the play—for example, when lawyer Demur expresses a regret that the law against Catholic priests in not enforced (p. 99). The lawyer's sentiments agree exactly with Centlivre's own as expressed in the Dedication to *The Gotham Election*.

The Artifice was published on October 27. Early in November a new periodical, the *Monthly Packet of Advices from Parnassus*, was launched. On November 7 an advertisement in the *Daily Journal*, signed "Susan Centlivre," defended *The Artifice* from an attack in the "Libel call'd *Advices from Parnassus*." This advertisement was subsequently disowned by "Susanna Cent Livre" in a letter published on November 22 in the *St. James's Journal*—a newspaper friendly to Centlivre that had carried a preproduction notice of *The Artifice*. The letter in the *St. James's Journal* denies any knowledge either of the origin of the advertisement in the *Daily Journal* or of the *Advices from Parnassus* mentioned in it. Since Centlivre nowhere else signs herself "Susan," suspicion naturally falls on the *Daily Journal* advertisement. Probably Edmund Curll, the publisher of *The Artifice*, was responsible for it. No doubt he thought that sales would be helped by any suggestion that the play was controversial.[18]

The *Monthly Packet of Advices from Parnassus* uses a device originated by the Italian satirist Trajano Boccalini in his *Ragguagli di Parnaso* (1612). The Court of Apollo tries and passes judgment on various cases that are brought before it. The *Monthly Packet* that attacks Centlivre is divided into three "Sessions." The first and second are directly concerned with religion and politics, and especially with defending the Non-Jurors. In the third session, the same concerns are thinly veiled in a debate that is at least nominally about literature and the arts.

The session begins with a lengthy account of the decline of the arts since the reign of Charles II. This theme is reinforced by the arrival of the nine muses as though from England. They confirm the present sorry state of the arts there. The political orientation of the discussion is illustrated by Clio's complaint that "another Piece is carefully plac'd in the Royal Library, where no Tory is permitted to enter, least he should find a Pedigree for one they call a Pretender."[19] Much the longest of the complaints is made by Thalia, the comic muse. Thalia's complaint—and Boccalini's defense of her—are an extended attack on *The Artifice*.[20]

The criticism of *The Artifice* is nominally literary, but the real object of the author's attack is political. In the style of Jeremy Collier, he objects that "the whole Scope of the Play is to encourage Adultery; to ridicule the Clergy; and to set Women, above the arbitrary Power of their Husbands."[21] This is a perverse reading of the play's intentions. Throughout, the author insists on treating *The Artifice* less as a play than as a moral tract. Of course it comes out badly. The *Monthly Packet* really tells us no more than that Centlivre's political enemies detested her as much as she detested them.

CHAPTER 8

Minor Writings

CENTLIVRE'S literary reputation rests entirely on her plays. Her nondramatic writings are chiefly of interest as personal documents; as sources of information about her life, character, and opinions. The few personal letters published in 1700 and 1701 tell us a little of the circumstances of her life at about the time of her arrival in London. The poems addressed to friends and acquaintances extend our knowledge of Centlivre's circle in later years. Other poems—the greater number—are public expressions of her political convictions and loyalties. Finally, there are a few lost works to be considered.

Perhaps the most interesting and enjoyable of these minor writings is the autobiographical poem *A Woman's Case* (1720). Addressed to a director of the South Sea Company before the collapse of the speculative bubble, it combines an appeal for patronage with a humorously engaging account of Centlivre's married life and money troubles.

I *Letters*

Centlivre must have written many letters during the course of her career, but no autograph manuscripts or even copies of them are known to survive. Only a few of her letters are still extant, preserved by the accident of contemporary publication. The reading public around 1700 had a keen appetite for collections of miscellaneous correspondence.[1] Two of Centlivre's early friends—Tom Brown and Abel Boyer—were among those who sought to gratify this public taste. Such collections as they edited typically included a mixture of new letters and old, English and translated, public and personal, witty and serious, moral and bawdy. The editors often took considerable liberties with their material. Fidelity to their originals was less important than giving the public entertaining and informative reading. Centlivre herself may have retouched and improved her letters for publication. Some of them may even have been written with publication half in mind. Their tone of studied negligence often suggests that this was the case.

Ironically enough, in a letter that was itself transparently intended for publication, we find Abel Boyer twitting Centlivre that " 'tis a great Reflection on your Vanity, that you should be at so great Expence of Wit and Humour, when you write for the Publick, and only fill your Letters with Business, when you write to your private Acquaintance."[2] But however self-conscious, these letters are as close as we can get to the style of Centlivre's familiar correspondence. Their prose style is naturally much less formal than that of the style of the dedications to her plays—which are in effect letters to her patrons. But in both the letters and the dedications, Centlivre's language is forceful rather than polished. There is little striving after verbal wit or clever writing. Boyer's "Wit and Humour" is opposed to "Business" and refers rather to content than to style.

Centlivre's first appearance in print was in a volume of *Familiar and Courtly Letters* by Voiture and others, edited by Tom Brown and published in May 1700. Seven letters to and from Centlivre are included. The first five are a set of conventional love letters between Centlivre and an anonymous correspondent. The second and fourth letters are from Centlivre. More interesting than the love letters are the last two in the group of seven. The first, dated April 8, 1700, is from Centlivre to Tom Brown himself and is a satirical account of a journey to Exeter in a stagecoach. Her fellow passengers illustrate conventional satirical themes: the corruption of elections, the boorishness of provincial life, and so on. In his reply, Brown urges her to return to London as soon as she can, since she is much missed among her friends.

A much longer correspondence involving Centlivre forms part of the *Letters of Wit, Politics, and Morality* edited by Abel Boyer and published in 1701. Boyer's was an unusually miscellaneous collection: "an extraordinary *olla podrida* of all kinds of letters new and old, translated and original."[3] It contained, among many others, the first English translations of Mme de Sévigné's letters. The correspondence with Centlivre falls into two groups. The first is a series of twenty-two letters between Celadon, Astraea (Centlivre), and Chloe (Celadon's mistress). Most of the letters are from Celadon; only six are from Astraea. They chart the progress—or rather the lack of progress—of relations between Celadon and Astraea. Celadon tries to interest Astraea in a sexual relationship, but she insists that they continue only as good friends. Halfway through the correspondence, Astraea learns about Chloe. The two women are soon on the best of terms. The most amusing part of the whole sequence is the episode (Letters 25–28) in which the two women join forces against Celadon. Celadon, as Bowyer argues, is probably the pseudonym of Captain William Ayloffe.[4] A shadowy figure of whom little is known, Ayloffe was a writer of sorts and a friend of Tom Brown's. He thus provides a link between Boyer's group and Brown's. Centlivre was evidently initmate with both groups.

The Celadon correspondence is followed by a group of assorted letters, more literary in flavor and content, between various members of the same circle. The sequence begins (Letter 38) with a letter from Boyer himself to Centlivre. It refers to Dryden's recent death and to Centlivre's own play—presumably *The Perjured Husband*. Boyer had been circulating the manuscript of this play around his friends with theatrical connections. Centlivre's reply (Letter 39) is probably the most interesting of all these early letters. In it she tells of her admiration for Dryden and Farquhar and expresses the view that "the main design of Comedy is to make us laugh."[5] She also gives a lively description of the small provincial town in which she is staying. Finally, she encloses a poem in praise of Farquhar and asks Boyer to pass it on to him. This poem evidently served as an introduction, for the next two letters are exchanged between Centlivre (Astraea) and Farquhar (Damon). These are in turn followed by a sequence of complimentary poems; two addressed to Farquhar by Centlivre, and one to Centlivre herself by Jane Wiseman. The group of letters is concluded by another from Boyer to Centlivre. In a strain of conventional gallantry, he admits that she has "gain'd a victor's Right o're me as well as Celadon."[6]

Tom Brown's collection of *Familiar and Courtly Letters* by Voiture and others was augmented by a second volume published in 1701. A section of contemporary letters called "A Pacquet from Will's"—the well-known coffeehouse—contains seven letters between Centlivre (Astraea) and Farquhar (confusingly using the pseudonym Celadon). Farquhar, like Ayloffe before him, tries to engage Centlivre in a physical intimacy. But Centlivre again rejects the idea, firmly but goodnaturedly: "I guess our Acquaintance will be but of a short Longitude," she writes in reply to a coarsely suggestive poem, "if your Pegasus take such a Latitude in his Stile. I am sorry you misunderstand my Intent, which was only to divert you over a Bottle, and my self from the Spleen."[7] Centlivre and Farquhar remained friends, however. In 1706, only a few months before he died, Farquhar wrote the Prologue for *The Platonic Lady*.

The Centlivre that emerges from these letters is a young woman determined to be independent and to make her own way in the man's world of literature without surrendering that independence. Her implicit demand as a correspondent is to be treated as a friend and an equal, not as a woman and, therefore, a potential mistress. She is an unaffected and intelligent woman of sense who will not coquet with men whom she means to refuse. We can recognize this character in the sensible women in her plays, from Clarinda in *The Beau's Duel* to Ann Lovely in *A Bold Stroke for a Wife*. It is true that in the letters Centlivre says no, and in the plays her heroines say yes. But they share a common belief in plain dealing in love.

No personal letters to or from Centlivre are known to survive from the later years of her career. But toward the end of her life, Centlivre contributed to the *Weekly Journal* a series of politicoreligious abstracts from the *Independent Whig*. These abstracts take the form of letters to the editor, and each abstract is prefaced by a sentence or two of Centlivre's own. The letters are signed "S.C." and were identified as Centlivre's by Paul Bunyan Anderson.[8] The author of the anonymous life prefixed to Centlivre's collected *Works* probably had these letters in mind when she wrote that "to reform the [Church], was our Author's latest Employ, and she shewed herself Mistress of the Subject in her Treatise which discloses and confutes the Errors of the Church of Rome."[9] If these letters were ever collected into a formal "Treatise"—which can hardly have been more than a pamphlet—it has not been traced.

Finally, there is the letter published in the *St. James's Journal* on November 22, 1722. This letter denies responsibility for the advertisement for *The Artifice* in the *Daily Journal* on November 7, and reaffirms Centlivre's loyalty to the king and the government. This is Centlivre's last known publication, and it is a spirited piece of work. In it, Centlivre attributes the attack on *The Artifice* in the *Monthly Packet of Advices from Parnassus* to "a turbulent Set of People, who finding their Schemes too weak to overturn the Government, vented their ill-manner'd Rage upon a Woman: and since they were not able to stab our Laws, and Liberties, they endeavoured to murder a poor Play."[10] In other words, the old coalition of Centlivre's enemies: the Tories, the Jacobites, and the Non-Jurors.

II *Poems*

Centlivre's poems span the whole of her writing career. Their forms are as various as their subject matter. They include elegies, odes, and epistles; they are written in heroic and octosyllabic couplets besides several stanza patterns; and they are addressed to recipients as different as the poet laureate and the king of Sweden. Yet most of these "poems" perform functions that prose has now largely taken over from verse. They are, for the most part, not expressive effusions but public statements.

The most personal of the poems are the complimentary verses addressed to Centlivre's friends and acquaintances. Besides the three to Farquhar published in *Letters of Wit, Politics, and Morality*, Centlivre addressed poems to Sarah Fyge Egerton, minor poet; to Ann Oldfield, the actress; to the Earl of Warwick; and to the Duchess of Bolton. Perhaps the most interesting of this group, for its theme rather than its verse, is the poem "To Mrs. S. F. on her Incomparable Poems." This was one of four sets of commendatory verses prefaced to Sarah Fyge's *Poems on Several Occasions* (1703). Centlivre urges Fyge to show "Ambitious Man what Womankind can do." The poem's praise of a well-educated woman looks forward to the treatment of Valeria in *The Basset Table* (1705).

More ambitious than any of the preceding are Centlivre's verse epistle to Nicholas Rowe and her pastoral elegy on his death. The epistle is "From the County to Mr. Rowe in Town." It is dated 1718, although it was not published until 1720, after Rowe's death. Its theme is the dullness and boorishness of country life. This admittedly well-worn topic—treated by Centlivre in prose in the *Letters of Wit, Politics, and Morality*—is competently and even wittily handled. By contrast, the elegy (1719) is tediously conventional. Amaryllis (Centlivre) mourns for Colin (Rowe) and laments his fate in the company of other rustic figures. Centlivre may also have written one of the elegies on Dryden's death published in *The Nine Muses* (1700). But the attribution of this poem is not certain. [11]

Besides these personal poems, Centlivre addressed several to public figures on occasions of national or political importance. The first of these was the poem to Prince Eugene of Savoy that was published with *The Perplexed Lovers* in 1712. Through an allegorical vision, Centlivre welcomes Eugene to Britain and takes at the same time a bellicose stand on the question of the peace negotiations then in progress.

Despite the anti-French sentiments expressed in the poem to Prince Eugene, Centlivre addressed a poem of welcome to the French envoy—the Duc d'Aumont—when he arrived in England the next year. But this poem is entirely apolitical—a courteous personal tribute to a visiting diplomat, not an endorsement of his political position. *The Masquerade* (1713) describes the various disguises assumed by the masquers and compliments D'Aumont on being able to "take no Form so lovely as his own."[12] Mottley tells an amusing story that links these two poems: "The Duke received her with great Politeness, when she went to wait upon him after sending her Poem, and asked if she had a Snuff-Box; she told him Yes, one that Prince Eugene had given her. Oh! said he, that was a Whig Box; now I will give a Tory Snuff-Box."[13]

Centlivre's evident satisfaction at the peaceful accession of George I was expressed in three poems published in November 1714. In *A Poem Humbly Presented to His Most Sacred Majesty*, George was hailed as England's deliverer from the "wicked race of Men" who misled the late Queen Anne. Another poem was addressed to the Earl of Halifax on his being made a Knight of the Garter. Centlivre complimented Halifax on his staunch patriotism and Whiggism. The third poem was a verse epistle to one of the ladies in waiting to the new Princess of Wales. *An Epistle to Mrs. Wallup* praised Princess Caroline as a worthy successor to Mary II, wife of William III. Queen Anne is pointedly omitted. Centlivre disliked Queen Anne not only for her Tory sympathies, but also for her failure to patronize the arts. Both Mary and Caroline had literary tastes, so that there is some justification for Centlivre's attitude. But like the other two poems, the *Epistle* is primarily an exuberant testimony to the strength of Centlivre's political convictions and to the real pleasure with which she greeted the Hanoverian dynasty. All three poems are in fact political rather than literary documents. Only in her plays—notably in *The Cruel Gift* and the two farces written in 1714—did Centlivre successfully subsume her political views into a genuinely literary achievement.

Centlivre's later public poems continue the same themes as those of 1714. The present happy reign is presented as a return to good King William's golden days after the bleak period of Tory rule under Queen Anne. Examples are the poems on St. George's Day, on the king's birthday, and the "Ode to Hygeia"—the last a poetic get well card addressed to Robert Walpole—of 1716. Slightly more personal are the two poems (also 1716) addressed to the Princess of Wales. But the most ambitious of these later poems is the *Epistle to the King of Sweden* (1717), in which Centlivre warns Charles XII of the folly of attacking England, happy and united under a prosperous reign. Centlivre's last poem was written for the anniversary of George I's coronation, in October 1722.

An interesting poem that is public in occasion but largely personal in content is *A Woman's Case* (1720). This poem is a verse epistle addressed to Charles Joye, a director of the South Sea company. It asks Joye to make her a present—as a reward for her loyal support of the Whig cause—of a block of the South Sea stock currently being offered by subscription. The poem's jerky but jaunty octosyllabics offer playful glimpses of life in the modest Centlivre household. Joseph Centlivre is presented as less than a keen Whig and as a less than uncritical admirer of his wife's literary efforts. This is his reaction to her decision in 1714 to dedicate *The Wonder* to the then Duke of Cambridge:

> Madam, said he, with surly Air,
> You've manag'd finely this Affair;
> Pox take your Schemes, your Wit, and Plays,
> I'm bound to curse 'em all my Days:
> If out, I'm by your Scribbling turn'd,
> I wish your Plays and you were burn'd.[14]

Susanna calms him by promising good times to come with the future George I. But when the Centlivres reap no personal advantage from the change of dynasty, Joseph resumes his complaints:

> Deuce take your scribling Vein, quoth he,
> What did it ever get for me?
> Two years you take a Play to write,
> And I scarce get my Coffe by't.
> Such Swingeing Bills are still to pay
> For Sugar, Chocolate, and Tea,
> I shall be forc'd to run away. (Pp. 7–8)

It is Joseph who suggests the expedient of writing to Joye, offering this inducement:

> If you prevail, I'll henceforth prove
> As faithful as a Turtle-Dove;
> Never hereafter will offend,

With either Male or Female Friend:
Write you to whom, or what you will,
Faith, I shall construe nothing ill. (P. 12)

We need not take the Joseph of the poem too literally or too seriously. But the disillusionment with the Whig regime—at least for its failure to reward the Centlivres adequately—that the poem expresses is a salutary corrective to Centlivre's optimism in her poems of 1714 and 1716. Evidently Centlivre believed that her services to Hanover deserved more than the royal command benefit performances she was given.

III   *Lost Works*

When Centlivre died in 1723, she left at least four poems in manuscript. Three were published between 1725 and 1732, and one is still in manuscript. It is difficult to infer what other works, left unpublished at Centlivre's death, may have been lost: possibly one or more uncompleted drafts of plays, certainly some letters, and at least one poem. There is the song which Giles Jacob reports that she had composed before she was seven years old.[15] Mottley also describes a later poem which seems to have been lost. This was addressed to the Duke of Newcastle: "a kind of Pastoral, which she had wrote upon his purchasing an Estate somewhere, and this was supposed to be a Welcome from the Nymphs and rural Inhabitants of the Place."[16]

A more interesting possibility is that Centlivre wrote an autobiography which has been lost. In 1732—and again in 1736—an edition of Centlivre's *Dramatical Works* was advertised as "in the Press." Besides her plays and poems, this was to contain "some Account of her Life and Writings. By her self."[17] According to J.E. Norton "a single copy of such an edition . . . has been seen in recent years but has been lost track of."[18] I have been unable to verify this or to locate a copy of the edition. Norton conjectures that the collection was to have been made up of sheets of separate reprints of individual plays, of which several are recorded at about this time. But not all the plays were reprinted—at least, I have not found copies of either *The Platonic Lady* or of *The Perplexed Lovers*—and the project may have been abandoned. But why the autobiography at least was not published is a mystery. Just possibly, the "some Account" was actually *A Woman's Case*, renamed by the publisher as an advertising gimmick. Certainly, if a set of these elusive *Dramatical Works* does turn up, and proves to contain an authentic autobiography, it will be a discovery of major importance.

CHAPTER 9

Conclusion

C ENTLIVRE'S career as a dramatist is a checkered record of trial
and error, of successes and failures, of compromises between
her artistic conscience and her desire for popular success. She
believed that the comic writer's first duty was to entertain, and she
was content to take her audience's tastes much as she found them. We
do not find in her prefaces and dedications—as we do in Dennis's—
complaints about the depraved and vitiated palates of theatergoers.
We do find occasional complaints about the middlemen of the drama,
the actors and the managers. The most notable instance is in the
Preface to *The Man's Bewitched*.[1] But in general, Centlivre saw the
collaboration of author and actor as a fruitful one. She wrote in the
Preface to *The Wonder* that "the Poet and the Player are like Soul and
Body, indispensibly necessary to one another; the correct Author
makes the Player shine, whilst the judicious Player makes the Poet's
fame immortal." The immortality that Centlivre sought was evidently
that of the theater rather than the library. This helps to explain why
she never collected or revised her plays as Congreve and even Cibber
did.

Paradoxically enough, for an author whose primary aim was to
entertain her countemporaries, Centlivre's plays—at least the best of
them—achieved their greatest popular success after her death. Her
most successful works in her own time were *The Gamester* and *The
Busy Body*. Both were regularly revived. *The Wonder, The Cruel
Gift*, and *A Bold Stroke for a Wife* had successful initial runs but did
not become stock pieces. But in the century or so after 1756, the year
in which Garrick first took the part of Felix in *The Wonder*,
Centlivre's three best plays—*The Busy Body, The Wonder*, and *A
Bold Stroke for a Wife*—were regularly reprinted and performed.
They held an assured place in the repertory of the popular theater.
Yet as Bowyer's study amply documents, Centlivre never acquired
much critical reputation. Hazlitt, for example, is a sympathetic critic

132

of Centlivre's comedies as he experienced them in the theater; but he is condescending to them as plays.[2]

After about 1880, Centlivre's plays gradually lost their place in the repertory, and they have been only very occasionally performed in this century. This rapid decline in popularity—rather surprising after they had survived so long—was a symptom of a major shift in theatrical taste. In 1953, Bertram Shuttleworth asked why Centlivre had not survived and suggested that it was "probably because we are no longer greatly interested in the plot of a play. . . . Centlivre gives us a plot, very little characterization, and rather flat, but unexpectedly natural diaglogue."[3] Certainly Centlivre's plays do not offer much of psychological interest. And yet when *The Busy Body* was revived at the Pitlochry Festival in 1973, the character of Sir Francis Gripe struck one reviewer as possessed of an intensity and a reality that reminded him of Shylock.[4] There are probably three or four Centlivre comedies into which an enterprising and thoughtful director could infuse life and vigor in the theater.

The general growth of scholarly and critical interest in restoration and eighteenth century drama is likely to result in Centlivre's plays being more widely read. She also has something to offer the feminist movement. The student of her plays certainly need make no special allowances on the score of Centlivre being a woman. But in the early eighteenth century there was an unthinking prejudice against women writers, and at certain points, Centlivre's career illustrates the difficulties that women had to contend with. The Dedication to *The Platonic Lady* is a dignified plea for equality of treatment that could well find a place in an anthology of early feminist writings.[5]

Our estimate of Centlivre's rank as a dramatist, and of the importance of her contribution to English literature, will naturally depend on how wide a perspective we choose to view her in. There can be no doubt of her historical importance. With Cibber, Steele, Farquhar, Vanbrugh, and Gay, Centlivre is one of the half-dozen comic dramatists of the early eighteenth century whose work still commands respect. Each of these playwrights made a distinct and individual—although not an equal—contribution to English comedy and its development.

Centlivre resisted the newer modes of comedy pioneered by Cibber and Steele and continued to write—although with many concessions to the "improved" moral tone of the times—in the tradition of the restoration comedy of intrigue with its distinctive blend of love and business. The story of Centlivre's successes and failures also illustrates the vagaries of public taste. Hers, then, is the representative career of a prolific, professional dramatist. For the student of early eighteenth century drama, Centlivre has therefore a double interest: for the expression of an individual comic vision, and also for the typical qualities of her art and her career.

In the wider perspective of English drama as a whole, however, Centlivre can rank only as a minor figure. She neither exerted the decisive influence on later comedy that Steele did nor achieved the permanent popularity that the best of Farquhar's plays have won. Centlivre's achievement should rather be compared with that of restoration dramatists of the second rank, such as Aphra Behn and John Crowne. It is true of all three that the greater part of their work is now of interest chiefly to the specialist. Yet each of these writers enriched English comedy with one or two plays of superior merit: we might single out Behn's *The Rover;* Crowne's *City Politics* and *Sir Courtly Nice;* and Centlivre's *The Busy Body* and *A Bold Stroke for a Wife.*

Centlivre's is an uneven achievement. Within certain limits, she was a lively experimenter with the various comic modes of her day. The problems and opportunities of the mixed genre seem especially to have fascinated her. *Marplot* and *The Artifice* are interesting in this way, although neither can be counted a success. But Centlivre also repeated herself, and some of her plays rely too heavily on stock situations and conventional characters. At her worst, Centlivre wrote the occasional routine potboiler. Much of her work is only mediocre. But at her best—in *The Busy Body* and *A Bold Stroke for a Wife*—she wrote amusing and lighthearted comedy of considerable distinction.

Notes and References

Chapter One

1. Giles Jacob, "Mrs. Susanna Centlivre," in *The Poetical Register* (London, 1719), pp. 31–32; Abel Boyer, Obituary of Centlivre in *The Political State of Great Britain*, 26 (December 1723), 670–71; John Mottley, "Mrs. Susanna Centlivre," in *A Complete List of All the English Dramatic Poets*, appended to Thomas Whincop, *Scanderbeg* (London, 1747), pp. 185–92; William Rufus Chetwood, "Mrs. Susanna Centlivre," in *The British Theatre* (Dublin, 1750), pp. 140–41. For a witty survey of these and other biographies, see James R. Sutherland, "The Progress of Error: Mrs. Centlivre and the Biographers," *Review of English Studies*, 17 (1942), 167–82. I have ignored the various later and derivative accounts.

2. Jacob, pp. 31–32.

3. Boyer, pp. 670–71.

4. John Wilson Bowyer, *The Celebrated Mrs. Centlivre* (Durham, N.C., 1952), pp. 92–93.

5. Mottley, p. 188.

6. Mottley, p. 185.

7. Mottley, p. 187.

8. Sutherland, p. 171.

9. Chetwood, p. 140.

10. Chetwood, p. 141.

11. John H. Mackenzie, "Susan Centlivre," *Notes and Queries*, 198 (September 1953), 386–90. But Mackenzie mistakenly took the Whaplode father to be the same man as the Freeman of Holbeach whose will was proved in 1674.

12. Bowyer, pp. 4–5.

13. Miss A. H. Cripps, archivist, Lincolnshire Archives Office, kindly checked the two documents for me and made the suggestion that the Susanna mentioned in the will was probably not a child at the time.

14. Bowyer, pp. 92–93.

15. Bowyer, pp. 244–45.

16. Bowyer, pp. 169–70, 221.

17. Samuel Johnson, Letter to Sir Joshua Reynolds, July 17, 1771; *Letters*, ed. R. W. Chapman (Oxford, 1952), I. 262.

18. Jacob, p. 301.

19. For details, see Bowyer, pp. 58, 98, 152, 208, 240. The original signed receipt for Curll's payments to Centlivre is extant. It is No. 68 in the

collection of the autographs of distinguished women assembled by William Upcott about 1825. The collection is now among the Evelyn papers on deposit in the library of Christ Church, Oxford.

20. Mottley, p. 191.

21. These figures are only guesstimates. For the early plays, I have assumed £10 from the publisher, £10 from the dedicatee, and £30 or more from each benefit. In 1698, Colley Cibber made about £114, £64, and £23 from his three benefit performances of *Woman's Wit* (Emmett L. Avery, *The London Stage, Part 2*, Carbondale, 1960, p. ci). It is not likely that Centlivre's receipts were on this scale before *The Wonder*, if at all. But for her later plays, she could count on being better known and on receiving some politically motivated support from Whig sympathisers.

22. About 1737 Samuel Johnson was assured "that thirty pounds a year was enough to enable a man to live [in London] without being contemptible"; James Boswell, *Life of Johnson*, ed. G. B. Hill, I (Oxford, 1934), 103-05.

23. Mottley, p. 188.

24. Bowyer, p. 93.

25. Besides the *Dictionary of National Biography*, two useful sources of information about the minor writers mentioned in this section are Pat Rogers, *Grub Street* (London, 1972); and James R. Sutherland's edition of *The Dunciad* (3rd ed., London, 1960), especially the Biographical Appendix. I have drawn from all three.

26. Bowyer, pp. 29–31.

27. Allardyce Nicoll, *A History of English Drama 1660–1900*, II (3rd ed., Cambridge, 1952), 159.

28. Mottley, p. 191.

29. Mottley, p. 191.

30. John Loftis, *The Politics of Drama in Augustan England* (Oxford, 1963), pp. 31–34.

31. Jacob, p. 32.

32. George Macaulay Trevelyan, *England under Queen Anne*, III (London, 1934), 202.

33. Mottley, p. 190.

34. George Farquhar,"A Discourse upon Comedy," *Complete Works*, ed. Charles Stonehill (Bloomsbury, 1930), II, 336.

35. Jeremy Collier, *A Short View of the Immorality and Profaneness of the English Stage* (London, 1698), p. 1.

36. John Loftis, *Comedy and Society from Congreve to Fielding* (Stanford, 1959), p. 65.

37. Pat Rogers, *The Augustan Vision* (London, 1974), p. 161.

38. William Congreve, "Concerning Humour in Comedy," reprinted in *Comedies*, ed. Bonamy Dobrée (London, 1925), p. 7. The essay—which takes the form of a letter to John Dennis—is dated 1695; it was published in a collection of *Letters on Several Occasions* edited by Dennis (London, 1696).

39. Congreve, p. 11.

40. *A Bold Stroke for a Wife*, ed. Thalia Stathas (Lincoln, Ne., 1968), p. 12.

41. Farquhar, II, 337.

42. This development is discussed in Stuart M. Tave, *The Amiable Humorist* (Chicago, 1960).

43. *The Man's Bewitched* (London, 1709), p. 48.

44. *The Artifice,* (London, 1723), p. 42.

45. George Sherburn, *The Early Career of Alexander Pope* (Oxford, 1934), pp. 163–65.

46. The poem is summarized in J. V. Guerinot, *Pamphlet Attacks on Alexander Pope* (London, 1969), pp. 38–40.

47. The pamphlets are reprinted in Alexander Pope, *Prose Works*, ed. N. Ault, I (Oxford, 1936), 257–66, 273–85.

48. *Prose Works*, p. 282

49. The case for Centlivre being the primary target is argued by George Sherburn, "The Fortunes and Misfortunes of *Three Hours after Marriage,*" *Modern Philology*, 24 (1926), 91–109. Bowyer (pp. 194–206) argues, less covincingly, for Lady Winchelsea. But even Bowyer accepts that "the burlesque of the drama of intrigue, the satire against translators, the relationship between Clinket and the players, and the cutting of her tragedy" (p. 206) refer specifically to Centlivre.

50. Bowyer, p. 205

51. *The Dunciad,* ed. Sutherland, pp. 146, 207.

52. Alexander Pope, *Correspondence*, ed. George Sherburn (Oxford, 1956), III, 352. The letter, written on Pope's behalf, is from the Earl of Peterborough to Lady Mary Wortley Montagu.

Chapter Two

1. Ben Jonson, Epilogue to *Cynthia's Revels* (1601), *Works*, ed. C. H. Herford and Percy Simpson, IV (Oxford, 1932), 183.

2. Samuel Johnson, "Prologue Spoken at the Opening of the Theatre in Drury-Lane, 1747," *Poems*, ed. E. L. McAdam, Jr. (New Haven, 1964), p. 89.

3. *Letters of Wit, Politicks, and Morality* (1701), Letter 38, Mr. B[oye]r to Astraea; reprinted in Farquhar, II, 258–59.

4. *The Perjured Husband* (London, 1700), pp. 35-37. Subsequent references are to this edition and will be given in the text.

5. "I am extremely concern'd for the loss of Apollo, for such I always thought Mr. Dryden. I have read his Works with Admiration; 'tis they that first inspir'd my feeble Genius, and fill'd my pleas'd fancy with Poetick Gingles." From Astraea's answer, Letter 39 in *Letters of Wit, Politicks and Morality*, reprinted in Farquhar, II, 260.

6. For Lessing's use of Centlivre, see Paul P. Kies, "The Sources and Basic Model of Lessing's *Miss Sara Sampson*," *Modern Philology*, 24 (1926), 65–90.

7. E. N. Hooker, "Charles Johnson's *The Force of Friendship* and *Love in a Chest:* A Note on Tragicomedy and Licensing in 1710," *Studies in Philology*, 34 (1937), 407–11.

8. John Dryden, *Of Dramatic Poesy and Other Essays*, ed. George Watson (London, 1962), I, 45. The subsequent quotations from Neander are on p. 59.

9. *The Beau's Duel* (London, 1702), pp. 40-42. Subsequent references are to this edition and will be given in the text.

10. John Harrington Smith, *The Gay Couple in Restoration Comedy* (Cambridge, Mass., 1948), pp. 198–203.

11. For these new proprieties, see Smith, pp. 199–201. The whole of Smith's Chapter 7 is also relevant to Centlivre and the change in comedy.

12. An insistance of irregular spacing on p. 40 (F4^V) could be the result of a press correction of Roarwell to Toper. It occurs in the fifth line at "to him, Toper is." There is excess space both before and after the comma. Roarwell is eliminated in the "Corrected" edition (London, 1715).

13. *A Comparison between the Two Stages*, ed. S. B. Wells (Princeton, 1942), p. 17. The *Comparison*, published anonymously, is sometimes attributed to Charles Gildon.

14. Thomas May, *The Heir*, reprinted in Robert Dodsley, *Select Collection of Old English Plays*, rev. ed. by W. Carew Hazlitt, XI (London, 1875). Jasper Mayne's *The City Match* is reprinted in the same collection, Vol. XIII.

15. May, pp. 527-28, 569-71, 561-63.

16. May, p. 521

17. May, p. 575.

18. Farquhar, I, 286.

19. *Love's Contrivance* (London, 1703), pp. 17-21. Subsequent references are to this edition and will be given in the text.

20. John Loftis *Comedy and Society from Congreve to Fielding*, p. 66. Loftis's whole discussion of Centlivre's treatment of the merchant (pp. 64–68) is illuminating.

21. F. W. Bateson, *English Comic Drama 1700–1750* (1929; reprinted New York, 1963) p. 72. Bateson made the comment on Centlivre's later plays.

Chapter Three

1. *Letters of Wit, Politicks, and Morality* (1701), Letter 39, Astraea to Mr. B[oye]r; reprinted in Farquhar II, 260.

2. Allardyce Nicoll, *A History of English Drama 1660–1900*, II, 282.

3. Richard Steele, *Plays*, ed. S. S. Kenny (Oxford, 1971), pp. 115,116.

4. Quoted in Steele, p. 104.

5. Steele, p. 104

6. Bowyer, p. 59.

7. This character type is analysed by Ben R. Schneider, "The Coquette-Prude as an Actress's Line in Restoration Comedy during the Time of Mrs. Oldfield," *Theatre Notebook,* 22 (1968), 143–56.

8. *The Gamester* (London, 1705), p. 60. Subsequent references are to this edition and will be given in the text.

9. Ernest Bernbaum, *The Drama of Sensibility* (Boston, 1915), p. 2 Bernbaum discusses *The Gamester* on pp. 98–100.

10. Arthur Sherbo, *English Sentimental Drama* (East Lansing, 1957), pp. 113–15. Important reservations about Sherbo's treatment of sentimental drama as a genre are expressed by John Loftis in his review in *Modern Language Notes,* 74 (1959), 447–50.

11. In *The Confederacy* (October 1705), Vanbrugh used Clarissa's plan to set up a basset table as an instance of the fashionable folly of city wives. But Clarissa's husband is at least a much richer man than shopkeeper Sago. Vanbrugh's treatment of the city is notably more astringent than Centlivre's.

12. *The Basset Table* (London, 1706), pp. 47-49. Subsequent references are to this edition and will be given in the text.

13. F. M. Smith, *Mary Astell* (New York, 1916), pp. 29–30.

14. Mary Astell, *A Serious Proposal to the Ladies* (London, 1694), p. 44.

15. Mottley, p. 188.

16. *The Laureat: or, The Right Side of Colley Cibber* (London, 1740), p.112. The anti-Cibber bias of this source makes its evidence suspect, however. For the activities of Grafton's Men, see Sybil Rosenfeld, *Strolling Players and Drama in the Provinces 1660-1750* (Cambridge, 1930, pp. 45–46, 169–70.

17. *An Apology for the Life of Colley Cibber,* ed. B. R. S. Fone (Ann Arbor, 1968), pp. 182–83. For a concise account of Cibber's plagiarism from Centlivre, see F. W. Bateson, *"The Double Gallant* of Colley Cibber," *Review of English Studies,* I (1925), 343–46.

18. Bellair is so spelled throughout the text, but he is Belair in the list of characters.

19. *Love at a Venture* (London, 1706), pp. 8-9. Subsequent references are to this edition and will be given in the text.

20. Thomas Corneille, *Théâtre complet,* ed. Edouard Thierry (Paris, 1881), pp. 291, 295.

21. The legal realities and comedy's cavalier treatment of them are discussed in G. S. Alleman, *Matrimonial Law and the Materials of Restoration Comedy* (Wallingford, Pa., 1942).

22. Belvil's real name is Beaumont; but to avoid confusion I have called him Belvil throughout. He is always so called in the play.

23. Alfred Harbage, *Cavalier Drama* (Cambridge, Mass., 1936), p. 36. Harbage summarizes the main features of the "Cavalier mode" on pp. 31–36.

Centlivre could also have found the mode in many restoration comedies.

24. *The Platonic Lady* (London, 1707), p. 17. Subsequent references are to this edition and will be given in the text.

25. The scene at the beginning of Act III (pp. 29–34) is partly translated from Regnard's *Attendez-moi sous l'orme* (1694), Scene vi. The opening scene of *The Platonic Lady* (pp. 1–4) is also partly translated from Scene i of *Attendez-moi sous l'orme*.

Chapter Four

1. Mottley, p. 189.

2. Mottley, p. 190.

3. *The Female Tatler*, No. 41 (October 7–10, 1709).

4. *The Tatler*, No. 15 (May 14, 1709); ed. G. A. Aitken, I (London, 1898), 135.

5. *The Tatler*, No. 19 (May 24, 1709); ed. Aitken, I, 163.

6. John Dryden, "To the Pious Memory of the Accomplisht Young Lady Mrs. Anne Killigrew, Excellent in the Two Sister-Arts of Poesie and Painting. An Ode," ll. 71–74; *Poems*, ed. James Kinsley (Oxford, 1958), I, 461.

7. *The Busy Body* (London, 1709), pp. 10-13, 19-23. Subsequent references are to this edition and will be given in the text.

8. William Wycherley, *Complete Plays*, ed. G. Weales (New York, 1967), p. 152.

9. Thomas Hobbes, *On Human Nature*, Chapter 9; in his *English Works*, ed. Sir W. Molesworth, IV (London, 1840), 46.

10. Tave, pp. 104, 105.

11. None of the "sources" are in fact very close. Bowyer discusses them (pp. 100–03) and sanely concludes that except for Jonson "her borrowings are general and no discredit to her" (p. 103).

12. John Downes, *Roscius Anglicanus* (London, 1706), p. 28.

13. Cibber, pp. 84-86.

14. Jess Byrd, Introduction to *The Busy Body* (Los Angeles, 1949), p. ii.

15. The time is inconsistently specified. In Act I (p. 10) it is given as ten minutes, but later (pp. 14, 19, 23) as an hour.

16. Ben Jonson, *Works*, eds. C. H. Herford, Percy and Evelyn Simpson, X (Oxford, 1950), 230. Jess Byrd (p. ii) thinks Centlivre's scene "a close imitation" of Jonson, but "more amusing . . . perhaps because the characters, especially Sir Francis Gripe and Miranda, are more credible and more fully portrayed."

17. These would all have been actual changes of scene, effected by changing the sliding flat scenes at the rear of the stage. The staging of Centlivre's plays is outside the scope of this study. The standard account is Richard Southern, *Changeable Scenery* (London, 1952). Southern does not mention Centlivre, but his work gives the contemporary practices.

18. Since this account was written, Robert D. Hume has discussed *The*

Busy Body as a type of "Augustan Intrigue Comedy" in *The Development of English Drama in the Late Seventeenth Century* (Oxford, 1976), pp. 116-21.

Chapter Five

1. Bowyer, p. 133.
2. A full account of this episode will be found in Bowyer, pp. 117–27. Bowyer quotes the relevant portions of the *Female Tatler*.
3. The suggestion was made by P. B. Anderson, "Innocence and Artifice: or, Mrs. Centlivre and the *Female Tatler*," *Philological Quarterly*, 16 (1937), 358–75. Bowyer rejects the case for Centlivre's authorship, although he thinks that she was at least indirectly responsible for the report about *The Man's Bewitched*.
4. *The Man's Bewitched* (London, 1709), p. 59. Subsequent references are to this edition and will be given in the text.
5. Despite the setting in Peterborough (north of London), the dialect used by the rustics seems to be southwestern. In Act III Slouch says, incongruously, "I'll stand by Master, for the honour of Zomersetshire" (p. 34). The dialect forms used are similar to those used by Isabella in *The Platonic Lady* for her Dorothy disguise. Dorothy is supposed to be fresh from Somerset.
6. Bowyer, p. 128.
7. The same collection also includes *The Guardians Overreached in their Own Humour*, a shortened version of *A Bold Stroke for a Wife*. H.R. Falk, "An Annotated Edition of Three Drolls from *The Strolers Pacquet Open'd* (1742)" (Ph. D. Thesis, Univ. of Southern California, 1970), suggests that the compiler-author of the drolls was the actor William Bullock, Sr. (pp. 71–85). Falk's thesis includes an annotated text of *The Guardians*, but not of *The Witchcraft of Love*.
8. Leo Hughes, *A Century of English Farce* (Princeton, 1956), p. 21.
9. On the first night only, the farce was advertised as *A Bickerstaff's Burial: or, Work for the Upholders*.
10. The play begins with a stage direction reminiscent of The Tempest: "A working Sea seen at a Distance, with the Appearance of a Head of a Ship bulging against a Rock: Mermaids rise and sing: Thunder and lightning: Then the Scene shuts" (p. 1). This is the only Centlivre play that uses such an elaborate piece of machinery.
11. *A Bickerstaff's Burying* (London, 1710), p. 23. Subsequent references are to this edition and will be given in the text.
12. *The Tatler*, No. 1 (April 12, 1709), ed. Aitken, I, 21.
13. *The Tatler*, No. 99 (November 26, 1709), ed. Aitken, II, 337.
14. Avery, p. 239. Puzzlingly, there is no "Wood" in *Marplot*. The "Wood" was presumably used to represent the Terriera de Passa. This was actually a public square, but Centlivre uses it as she had St. James's Park in *The Busy Body*. Boul's scene may have been commissioned not with *Marplot*

in mind, but in response to competition from the rival opera company at the Queen's Theater. *Pyrrhus and Demetrius* had been advertised on December 16 "with the Addition of a New Cascade Scene after the Italian Manner" (Avery, p. 238). Evidently, Italian pastoral scenes were good box office.

15. For England's relations with Portugal at this time, see A.D. Francis, *The Methuens and Portugal 1691-1708* (Cambridge, 1966).

16. Dryden, *Of Dramatic Poesy and Other Critical Essays*, I, 244. For a thorough discussion of the "Spanish" plot, see John Loftis, *The Spanish Plays of Neoclassical England* (New Haven, 1973). By Centlivre's time, the "Spanish" plot was a domesticated convention of the English stage.

17. *Marplot* (London, 1711), pp. 38–39. Subsequent references are to this edition and will be given in the text. The pagination is irregular; in references the designation "51b" is used to indicate the second page so numbered.

18. Centlivre has a similar problem with divided sympathies in the character of Ned Freeman in *The Artifice*. Like Charles, Ned is involved in both a comic intrigue and a serious plot aimed at reforming him.

19. *The Perplexed Lovers* (London, 1712), pp. 1–4, 12–14. Subsequent references are to this edition and will be given in the text.

Chapter Six

1. *The Lover*, No. 27 (April 27, 1714); in *Periodical Journalism 1714–16*, ed. Rae Blanchard (Oxford, 1959), pp. 101, 100.

2. *The Wonder* (London, 1714), pp. 29–32. Subsequent references are to this edition and will be given in the text.

3. Edward Ravenscroft, *The Wrangling Lovers* (London, 1677), pp. 17–20, 65–69. See also Bowyer, pp. 172–76.

4. I have replaced the original commas with colons after "Discipline" and "Lists."

5. Loftis, *Comedy and Society from Congreve to Fielding*, p. 88.

6. The refusal of the license is reported in Centlivre's Dedication. For the patent and Drury Lane's subsequent independence of the Lord Chamberlain's office, see John Loftis, *Steele at Drury Lane* (Berkeley, 1952), pp. 48–49. Until Lincoln's Inn Fields reopened on December 18, 1714, Drury Lane was the only theater in London. In addition, the list of characters in *A Wife Well Managed* lists the actors who were to have taken the parts; they are from the Drury Lane company. *A Wife Well Managed* was subsequently staged in 1724; *The Gotham Election* seems never to have been acted.

7. They were advertised as "Two very Diverting Farces" in the *Monthly Catalogue*, II, No. 2 (Books published in June 1715). They were also issued separately. The Preface was probably written shortly before publication, since it refers to Rowe's *Lady Jane Grey*, which was first produced on April 20, 1715.

8. *A Wife Well Managed* (London, 1715), pp. 17–18.

9. Bowyer, pp. 165–66.

10. *Oxford English Dictionary, s.v.* "Gotham".

11. A[ndrew] B[orde], *The Merry Tales of the Mad Men of Gotham* (London, 1620), p. 5. The attribution to Borde is not certain. The name Gotham is variously spelled.

12. *The Examiner,* IV, No. 37 (October 9–12, 1713). See also Loftis, *Steele at Drury Lane,* p. 238.

13. *The Lover,* No. 11 (March 20, 1714), in *Periodical Journalism,* pp. 39–42. The satire is continued in later papers: Nos. 14, 16, and 21.

14. Tickup's failure to find a running mate emphasizes his isolation. But such three-cornered contests between two parties were not uncommon. In Winchester in 1715, George Bridges and Lord William Powlet (Whig) stood against John Popham (Tory). This example is taken from W.A. Speck, *Tory and Whig: The Struggle in the Constituencies 1701–15* (London, 1970), p. 125.

15. *The Gotham Election* (London, 1715), pp. 25–32. Subsequent references are to this edition and will be given in the text.

16. Mottley, p. 191. Mottley's memory is at fault here: none of the acts ends in such a way. There is a simile involving a halcyon (p. 50), but it describes the bird abandoning its nest during a flood, not building it on a fine day.

17. *A Satyr upon the Present Times* (London, 1717), p. 16. Published anonymously.

18. *The Cruel Gift* (London, 1717), pp. 54–57. Subsequent references are to this edition and will be given in the text.

19. His identity as duke of Milan is connected with the play's complicated political prehistory, which I have omitted in the interest of brevity.

20. On the sources, see further Bowyer, pp. 211–12.

21. John Dennis, *Remarks upon Cato* (1713), in *Critical Works,* ed. E.N. Hooker, II (Baltimore, 1943), 47.

22. Joseph Addison, *The Spectator,* No. 40 (April 16, 1711); ed. D.F. Bond (Oxford, 1965), I, 171.

23. John Dryden, "Sigismonda and Guiscardo, from Boccace," *Poems,* IV, 1545.

24. Loftis, *The Politics of Drama in Augustan England,* pp. 155, 161.

Chapter Seven

1. *A Bold Stroke for a Wife,* ed. Thalia Stathas (Lincoln, Ne., 1968), p. 18. Subsequent references are to this edition and will be given in the text.

2. Mottley, p. 191.

3. These are discussed by Thalia Stathas in the Introduction to her edition of *A Bold Stroke for a Wife,* pp. xvi-xvii.

4. John Genest, *Some Account of the English Stage from the Restoration in 1660 to 1830* (Bath, 1832), II, 498–99. See also Bowyer, p. 214.

5. See E.K. Maxfield, "The Quakers in English Plays before 1800,"

PMLA, 45 (1930), 256–73. Maxfield, however, overlooked *A Bold Stroke for a Wife;* see Bowyer, *PMLA,* 45 (1930), 957–58.

6. *The Lover,* No. 16 (April 1, 1714); in *Periodical Journalism 1714–16,* pp. 58–61. See also *The Lover,* Nos. 11, 14, and 21.

7. John Gay, Alexander Pope, and John Arbuthnot, *Three Hours After Marriage,* in *Burlesque Plays of the Eighteenth Century,* ed. Simon Trussler (London, 1969), p. 130.

8. John Tradescant, *Musaeum Tradescantiarum* (1656); reprinted in Mea Allan, *The Tradescants* (London, 1964), pp. 252, 266, 268.

9. Loftis, *Comedy and Society from Congreve to Fielding,* p. 95.

10. Daniel Defoe, *The Anatomy of Exchange-Alley* (London, 1719), p. 3. The pamphlet was published anonymously.

11. William Taverner, *The Female Advocates* (London, 1713), p. 19. Published anonymously.

12. Introduction, *A Bold Stroke for a Wife,* ed. Stathas, p. xix.

13. Avery, p. 569, cites this report, but wrongly gives the title of the play as *The Sacrifice.*

14. The Dedication is reprinted in John Dennis, *Critical Works,* II, 176–80. See also Loftis, *Steele at Drury Lane,* pp. 133–34.

15. *The Artifice* (London, 1723), pp. 20–30. Subsequent references are to this edition and will be given in the text.

16. Subscriptions to the *Monthly Packet of Advices from Parnassus* were invited in an advertisement in the *Post Boy* for November 1–3, 1722. I have only seen the number that contains the attack on *The Artifice* (British Library, 517.g.42). Perhaps this was the only one published. The pamphlet seems to be very scarce; it eluded Bowyer's search (p. 241). It was published anonymously, but in *The Early Career of Alexander Pope* (Oxford, 1934) George Sherburn conjectured that the author might be Matthias Earbury (p. 305).

17. *A Monthly Packet of Advices from Parnassus* (London, 1722), p. 32.

18. The imprint on the title-page is "Printed for T. Payne." But according to a receipt in Curll's hand (see above, Chapter 1, note 5), he, Mears, and Payne had each a third share in *The Artifice.* The advertisement in the *Daily Journal* is in the names of Curll and Payne. For Curll's typical publicity tricks, see Ralph Straus, *The Unspeakable Curll* (London, 1927).

19. *Monthly Packet,* p. 30.

20. *Monthly Packet,* pp. 31–35.

21. *Monthly Packet,* p. 33.

Chapter Eight

1. See W. H. Irving, *The Providence of Wit in the English Letter Writers* (Durham, N. C., 1955), ch. 3.

2. *Letters of Wit, Politicks, and Morality* (1701) ed. Boyer; reprinted in Farquhar II, 259.

3. Irving, p. 134.

4. Bowyer, pp. 20–21.

5. Farquhar, II, 260.

6. Farquhar, II, 268.

7. Farquhar, II, 231.

8. Anderson, p. 375.

9. *Works*, I (London, 1761), xi. The anonymous author describes herself as a woman (p. vii).

10. *St James's Journal*, November 22, 1722, p. 179.

11. Bowyer, pp. 31–33.

12. *The Masquerade* (London, 1713), p. 7.

13. Mottley, p. 191.

14. *A Woman's Case* (London, 1720), p. 3.

15. Jacob, p. 32.

16. Mottley, p. 192.

17. The advertisement appeared in editions of William Taverner's *The Maid the Mistress* published by Feales in 1732 and 1736.

18. J. E. Norton, "Some Uncollected Authors, xiv: Susanna Centlivre," *The Book Collector*, 6 (1957), 284.

Chapter Nine

1. Even here, the complaint is not about poor acting but about the arbitrary suppression of the play from pique.

2. See William Hazlitt, *Complete Works*, ed. P. P. Howe (London, 1930), V, 155–56; and VI, 332–33.

3. Bertram Shuttleworth, Review of Bowyer, *Theatre Notebook*, 8 (1953), 20.

4. George Bruce, "Comical Contrivance," *The Sunday Times*, July 15, 1973, p. 37.

5. Since this was written, the Dedication to *The Platonic Lady* has been reprinted in *The Female Spectator: English Women Writers before 1800*, ed. Mary R. Mahl and Helene Koon (Bloomington, In., 1977), pp. 215–16.

Selected Bibliography

PRIMARY SOURCES

1. Collected Works

Dramatical Works. 4 vols. London, 1732 (?), 1736 (?). Advertised as "in the Press" in William Taverner, *The Maid the Mistress* (London, 1732 and 1736). No copy located; perhaps never published.

Four Celebrated Comedies. London, 1735. Includes *The Beau's Duel, The Basset Table, A Bold Stroke for a Wife,* and *The Artifice.* A reissue of separate reprints of the four plays with a general title page.

The Works of the Celebrated Mrs. Centlivre. 3 vols. London, 1760–61. Includes only the plays. *Marplot* is represented by the shortened version, *Marplot in Lisbon.*

The Dramatic Works of the Celebrated Mrs. Centlivre. 3 vols. London, 1872. A type facsimile reprint of the *Works.*

"A Critical Edition of Three Plays by Susanna Centlivre." Ed. Thalia Stathas. Ph. D. diss., Stanford Univ., 1965. Includes *The Busy Body, The Wonder,* and *A Bold Stroke for a Wife,* with textual and explanatory notes.

2. Plays

The Perjur'd Husband: or, The Adventures of Venice. London, 1700.

The Beau's Duel: or, A Soldier for the Ladies. London, 1702. Pages misnumbered: 1–51, 53, 54, 54, 55.

The Stolen Heiress: or, The Salamanca Doctor Outplotted. London, [1703].

Love's Contrivance: or, Le Medecin malgre lui. London, 1703.

The Gamester. London, 1705.

The Basset-Table. London, 1706.

Love at a Venture. London, 1706.

The Platonick Lady. London, 1707.

The Busie Body. London, [1709].

———. Reprinted. Los Angeles, 1949, with an Introduction by Jess Byrd (Augustan Reprint Society, No. 19).

The Man's Bewitched: or, The Devil to Do about Her. London, [1709].

A Bickerstaff's Burying: or, Work for the Upholders. London, [1710].

Mar-Plot: or, The Second Part of the Busie Body. London, 1711. Pages misnumbered: 1–40, 49–56, 49–62.

The Perplex'd Lovers. London, 1712.

The Wonder: A Woman Keeps a Secret. London, 1714.

The Gotham Election. London, 1715.

A Wife Well Manag'd. London, 1715. Also published with *The Gotham Election* as *Two Farces* (London, 1715).

The Cruel Gift. London, 1717. The running title is "The Cruel Gift: or, The Royal Resentment."

A Bold Stroke for a Wife. London, 1718.

———. Ed. Thalia Stathas. Lincoln: University of Nebraska Press, 1968 (Regents Restoration Drama Series). Critical edition, with Introduction, textual and explanatory notes.

The Artifice. London, 1723.

3. Poems

"On the Death of John Dryden." In *The Nine Muses.* London, 1700. The attribution to Centlivre of the poem by "Polumnia" is doubtful.

"To Mr. Farquhar upon his Comedy call'd *A Trip to the Jubilee*"; "An Epistle in Verse. Astraea to Damon"; and "A Copy of Verses. Shut up in a Snuf-Box." In *Letters of Wit, Politicks, and Morality.* Ed. Abel Boyer. London, 1701.

"To Mrs. S. F. on her Incomparable Poems." In *Poems on Several Occasions.* By Mrs. S[arah] F[yge]. London, [1703].

"To his Illustrious Highness Prince Eugene of Savoy." Appended to *The Perplex'd Lovers* (London, 1712), pp. 56–60.

The Masquerade. London, 1713. Published with French prose translation.

"To the Army." In *Poetical Merriment: or, Truths Told to Some Tune.* London, 1714. Centlivre's poem is in the Supplement to Part III, dated 1713.

A Poem Humbly Presented to His Most Sacred Majesty George [etc]. London, 1715. Published November 1714.

An Epistle to Mrs. Wallup [etc]. London, 1715. Published November 1714.

"On the Right Hon. Charles Earl of Halifax Being Made Knight of the Garter." *The Patriot*, November 16–18, 1714.

"To Her Royal Highness the Princess of Wales." *The Patriot*, January 15–18, 1715.

"Invocation to Juno Lucina for the Safe Delivery of Her Royal Highness the Princess of Wales." *The Protestant Packet*, January 21, 1716.

"Upon the Bells Ringing at St. Martins in the Fields on St. George's Day 1716." *The Flying Post*, May 10–12, 1716.

"Ode to Hygeia." In *State Poems.* London, 1716.

"These Verses were Writ on King George's Birth-Day [etc]." In *A Collection of State Songs, Poems, etc.* London, 1716.

An Epistle to the King of Sweden from a Lady of Great Britain. London, 1717.

"A Pastoral to the Honoured Memory of Mr. Rowe." In *Musarum Lachrymae: or, Poems to the Memory of Nicholas Rowe.* London, 1719.

"To the Dutchess of Bolton upon Seeing Her Picture Drawn Unlike Her"; "To the Earl of Warwick on His Birthday"; and "From the Country to

Mr. Rowe in Town, MDCCXVIII." In *A New Miscellany of Original Poems, Translations and Imitations*. Ed. A[nthony] H[ammond]. London, 1720.

A Woman's Case: In an Epistle to Charles Joye, Esq: Deputy-Governor of the South-Sea. London, 1720.

"Letter on the Receipt of a Present of Cyder." In *A Miscellaneous Collection of Poems, Songs, and Epigrams*. Ed. T. M., Dublin, 1721.

Untitled poem on the anniversary of George I's coronation. *The Weekly Journal*, October 20, 1722.

Untitled poem addressed to Isaac Bickerstaff. In *Original and Genuine Letters Sent to the Tatler and Spectator*. Ed. Charles Lillie. 2 vols. London, 1725. Centlivre's poem is in Volume II.

Untitled poem written on the flyleaf of Mrs. Oldfield's copy of Fontenelle's *Plurality of Worlds*. In *Faithful Memoirs of . . . Mrs. Anne Oldfield*. By William Egerton [probably a pseudonym for Edmund Curll]. London, 1731.

Untitled poem addressed to a Whig, asking him to attend a benefit performance. *Carribeana*, September 6, 1732.

"A Poem on the Recovery of the Lady Henrietta Hollis from the Small Pox." Nonautograph manuscript. British Library. Harleian MS. 7649 (2).

4. Letters

In *Familiar and Courtly Letters Written by Monsieur Voiture* [etc]. London, 1700.

In *Familiar Letters by Monsieur Voiture* [etc]. London, 1701. Vol. II of above.

In *Letters of Wit, Politicks, and Morality* [etc]. London, 1701.

In *The Weekly Journal: or, British Gazetteer*. September to December 1720. A series of abstracts from *The Independent Whig*, each with a very brief introduction.

In *The St. James's Journal*. November 22, 1722. Letter disowning the advertisement for *The Artifice* in the *Daily Journal* for November 7.

SECONDARY SOURCES

ALLEMAN, GELLERT S. *Matrimonial Law and the Materials of Restoration Comedy*. Wallingford, Pa.: no publisher, 1942. Alleman "attempts to provide the background for those legal materials which the comic dramatists use most frequently" (p. 144). Centlivre is the "most frequent user of the clandestine marriage," but below average in the use of the tricked and mock marriage (p. 82).

ANDERSON, PAUL BUNYAN. "Innocence and Artifice: or, Mrs. Centlivre and *The Female Tatler*." *Philological Quarterly*, 16 (1937), 358–75. Attempts to identify the later issues of the *Female Tatler* as a collaboration between Centlivre and Mandeville. For counterarguments see Bowyer, pp. 117–32.

AVERY, EMMETT L. *The London Stage 1660–1800. Part 2, 1700–1729.* 2 vols. Carbondale: Southern Illinois University Press, 1960. The Introduction gives a comprehensive account of the contemporary theater; the main body of the work is a calendar of daily performances.

BATESON, F. W. *English Comic Drama 1700–1750.* Oxford, 1929; reprinted New York: Russell and Russell, 1963. Chapter 4 gives a brief critical survey of Centlivre's plays.

BERNBAUM, ERNEST. *The Drama of Sensibility.* Boston: Ginn, 1915. Includes a brief but illuminating study of *The Gamester;* a good overall account of "sentimental" comedy.

BOWYER, JOHN WILSON. *The Celebrated Mrs. Centlivre.* Durham, N.C.: Duke University Press, 1952. A thorough and detailed study, including sources, biographical evidence, and stage histories of the plays. Also valuable for its copious extracts from Centlivre's poems and letters. Weakest in its treatment of critical problems, but still the most important single source for the study of Centlivre. Based on Bowyer's Harvard dissertation (1928).

BOYER, ABEL. Obituary of Centlivre in *The Political State of Great Britain,* 26 (December 1723), 670–71. A valuable testimony by a man who had known Centlivre, but factually inaccurate.

CHETWOOD, WILLIAM RUFUS. "Mrs. Susanna Centlivre." In *The British Theatre.* Dublin, 1750. A brief account that probably preserves some authentic biographical details.

CIBBER, COLLEY. *An Apology for the Life of Colley Cibber* (1740). Ed. B. R. S. Fone. Ann Arbor: University of Michigan Press, 1968. An eclectic and fascinating account of its subject and also of the London stage in Centlivre's time.

CONGREVE, WILLIAM. "Concerning Humour in Comedy." In *Letters upon Several Occasions* [by Dryden and others]. London, 1696. Reprinted in *Comedies,* ed. Bonamy Dobrée (London: Oxford University Press, 1925), pp. 1–11. A classic account of "humour"; Congreve gives it a narrower meaning than Centlivre does in her dramatic practice.

CRAIK, T. W., ed. *The Revels History of Drama in English. Volume V, 1660–1750.* London: Methuen, 1976. A composite history, with sections on "The Social and Literary Context" by John Loftis, "Theatres and Actors" by Richard Southern and Marion Jones, and "Plays and Playwrights" by A. H. Scouten. The account of Centlivre (pp. 234–35) is disappointingly brief, but the book provides a useful general survey.

DRYDEN, JOHN. *Of Dramatic Poesy and Other Critical Essays.* Ed. George Watson. 2 vols. (Everyman's Library.) London: Dent, 1962. The most useful body of contemporary critical writing on the drama. Illustrates the critical tradition in which Centlivre wrote.

FARQUHAR, GEORGE. "A Discourse upon Comedy in Reference to the English Stage." *Love and Business.* London, 1702. Reprinted in *Complete Works,* ed. Charles Stonehill (Bloomsbury: Nonesuch Press, 1930). Expresses a view of comedy close to Centlivre's own; see her Preface to *Love's Contrivance* (1703).

HOLMES, GEOFFREY. *British Politics in the Age of Anne.* London: Macmillan, 1967. A detailed account of the workings of politics in the period that formed Centlivre's political views.

HUGHES, LEO. *A Century of English Farce.* Princeton: Princeton University Press, 1956. General critical account of the nature and rise of farce in the restoration and early eighteenth century.

HUME, ROBERT D. *The Development of English Drama in the Late Seventeenth Century.* Oxford: Clarendon Press, 1976. Contains many incidental references to Centlivre, and a discussion of *The Busy Body* as a type of "Augustan Intrigue Comedy". A valuable study of the period up to 1710. Hume's emphasis on the formulaic nature of the comic drama is particularly helpful in the evaluation of Centlivre's comedies.

IRVING, WILLIAM HENRY. *The Providence of Wit in the English Letter Writers.* Durham, N.C.: Duke University Press, 1955. Chapter 3 provides the historical context for an understanding of the collections of letters to which Centlivre contributed.

JACOB, GILES. "Mrs. Susanna Centlivre." In *The Poetical Register: or, The Lives and Characters of the English Dramatic Poets.* London, 1719. An "authorized" account, with the value and limitations that that implies.

KNAPP, MARY E. *Prologues and Epilogues of the Eighteenth Century.* New Haven: Yale University Press, 1961. General critical study of these indispensable adjuncts of a play. Many references to Centlivre's prologues and epilogues.

KRUTCH, JOSEPH WOOD. *Comedy and Conscience after the Restoration.* New York: Columbia University Press, 1924; rpt. 1949 with Preface, Bibliography, and Index. A critical study of the Collier controversy, its background, and its aftermath. Includes a critique of *The Artifice* (pp. 121–22).

LOFTIS, JOHN. *Comedy and Society from Congreve to Fielding.* Stanford: Stanford University Press, 1959. A critical study of comedy's changing social attitudes. Centlivre emerges as a representative transitional figure.

―――. *The Politics of Drama in Augustan England.* Oxford: Clarendon Press, 1963. Traces the connections between politics and the theater. Incidental treatment of Centlivre.

―――. *The Spanish Plays of Neoclassical England.* New Haven: Yale University Press, 1973. Chapters 4 and 5 and discuss the "Spanish plots" that are ultimately the origins of Centlivre's "Spanish" plays: *Marplot, The Perplexed Lovers,* and *The Wonder.*

MACKENZIE, JOHN H. "Susan Centlivre." *Notes and Queries,* 198 (Sep-

tember 1953), 386–90. Discovery of Centlivre's probable date and place
of birth, with a useful summary of other biographical evidence.

A Monthly Packet of Advices from Parnassus. London, 1722. Only one issue
published (?). Contains a detailed—but largely political—attack on *The
Artifice.*

MOTTLEY, JOHN. "Mrs. Susanna Centlivre." *A Compleat List of All the
English Dramatic Poets.* Appended to Thomas Whincop, *Scanderbeg*
(London, 1747). An entertaining but unreliable account of Centlivre's
life and writings. Probably preserves authentic information about
Centlivre's later years, when Mottley knew her.

NICOLL, ALLARDYCE. *Early Eighteenth-Century Drama.* Cambridge: Cambridge University Press, 1925. Rev. ed., 1952, as Vol. II of his *History of
English Drama 1660–1900.* Rather out of date critically, but retains
value as a fairly inclusive survey.

NORTON, J. E. "Some Uncollected Authors, XIV: Susanna Centlivre." *The
Book Collector,* 6 (1957), 172–78, 280–85. Supplemented by three notes
in later issues of *The Book Collector:* by Alan D. McKillop, 7 (1958),
79–80; by D. G. Neill, 7 (1958), 189–90; and by Jacqueline Fauré, 10
(1961), 68–69. Detailed bibliographical descriptions of the first editions,
with transcriptions of title pages. Also records newspaper advertise-
ments of the publication of Centlivre's works.

ROGERS, PAT. *Grub Street: Studies in a Subculture.* London: Methuen,
1972. Provides some interesting contexts and much miscellaneous
information. Centlivre did a small niche in this subculture.

SCHNEIDER, BEN R. "The Coquette-Prude as an Actress's Line in Restoration Comedy during the Time of Mrs. Oldfield." *Theatre Notebook,* 22
(1968), 143–56. An interesting study of a type of character found in
several of Centlivre's plays; also of more general interest for its
conclusions about casting practices.

SHERBO, ARTHUR. *English Sentimental Drama.* East Lansing: Michigan
State University Press, 1957. Includes a brief discussion of *The Gamester.* I have found it less persuasive than Bernbaum as an account of
"sentimental" drama.

SHERBURN, GEORGE. "The Fortunes and Misfortunes of *Three Hours after
Marriage.*" *Modern Philology,* 24 (1926), 91–109. Argues the case for
Centlivre as the primary target of the satirical portrait of Phoebe Clinket
in the play.

SMITH, JOHN HARRINGTON. *The Gay Couple in Restoration Comedy.*
Cambridge, Mass.: Harvard University Press, 1948. Smith's analysis of
the development and decline of the "gay couple" is relevant to
Centlivre's use of contrasting pairs of heros and heroines.

SPECK, W. A. *Tory and Whig: The Struggle in the Constituencies 1701–1715.*
London: Macmillan, 1970. Complements Holmes's study—listed
above—with an account of how politics worked at the local level.
Particularly illuminating as a background for *The Gotham Election.*

STROZIER, ROBERT. "A short View of Some of Mrs. Centlivre's Celebrat'd Plays, including a Close Accounting of the Plots, Subplots, Asides, Soliloquies, Etcetera, Contain'd Therein." *Discourse*, 7 (1964), 62–80. An insensitive study of an arbitrary selection of seven plays. Critical comments marred by a failure to see Centlivre's plays in the context of contemporary drama and its conventions.

SUTHERLAND, JAMES R. "The Progress of Error: Mrs. Centlivre and the Biographers." *Review of English Studies*, 17 (1942), 167–82. A discussion of the biographical evidence. Sutherland's sane and sceptical approach is a good corrective to Bowyer's more credulous account.

TAVE, STUART M. *The Amiable Humorist: A Study of the Comic Theory and Criticism of the Eighteenth and Early Nineteenth Centuries*. Chicago: University of Chicago Press, 1960. Provides the necessary contexts for an understanding of Centlivre's use of "humor" characters.

WILSON, JOHN HAROLD. *A Preface to Restoration Drama*. Boston: Houghton Mifflin, 1965. A good introduction to Centlivre's dramatic inheritance. Chapter 12 includes a sympathetic discussion of the comedy of intrigue and its relation to farce.

Index